# DIVINING ᵀᴴᴱ
# DOW

## 100 OF THE WORLD'S MOST WIDELY FOLLOWED STOCK MARKET PREDICTION SYSTEMS

## RICHARD J. MATURI

**PROBUS PUBLISHING COMPANY**
**Chicago, Illinois**
**Cambridge, England**

ISBN 1-55738-475-4

Printed in the United States of America

BB

2  3  4  5  6  7  8  9  0

*Richard J. Molini*

# Dedication

To our very special friends,
Fred and Roz,
who have enriched our lives.

# Contents

# Preface

There are a myriad of investment books that specialize in discussing one, two, or a half dozen investment predictors, indicators, theories and/or strategies. What I have attempted to produce with *Divining the Dow* is a handy desk reference that provides the investor with a comprehensive listing and a brief description of a broad variety of such predictors, indicators, theories, and strategies.

This reference will provide an excellent starting point in your search to develop a successful investment strategy. As you develop interest in a certain area, you can refer to other Probus Publishing books for more in-depth treatments of the subjects.

Where there is ongoing debate as to the merits of a particular topic, I have tried to present an unbiased view of both sides of the argument. As an astute investor, you can make your own judgment how, and if, it fits into your own investment perspective.

Many of the topics covered in this book are interrelated and realistically could have been included in any one of several chapters. I have included references where appropriate. Feel free to flip back and forth in order to deepen your understanding of these relationships and to strengthen your own investment strategy.

Finally, if you think of other investment topics to cover, drop the publisher a note with some details and we will cover it in the revised edition.

Richard J. Maturi
Cheyenne, Wyoming
1993

## Acknowledgement

I wish to thank the following, who were kind enough to supply charts to help illustrate this book:

Dreman Value Management, L.P.
*Investor's Business Daily*
New York Stock Exchange, Inc.

# 1

# The Economic Playing Field

In order to put individual stock market prediction systems into perspective, a review of the overall economic playing field is in order. Investment strategies do not operate in a vacuum and a good grounding in economic cycles and time cycles will prove beneficial as we investigate individual investment strategies in more detail in following sections.

## ECONOMIC CYCLES

Economic cycles are tied directly to changing economic conditions such as such bond prices, commodity availability and prices, interest rates, inflation, money supply, etc. In addition, economic cycles can also be impacted from forces initially outside the economic arena such as wars, political climate (both domestic and international), trade policies, etc. Economic cycles tend to play themselves out over long time periods.

1

### The Kondratieff Wave

We owe the origin of one of the most noted early studies of economic and market cycles, not to the centers of capitalist activity, but to the Union of Soviet Socialist Republics' regime under Premier Vladimir Lenin. Nikolai D. Kondratieff, a Russian economist, founded and oversaw the operations of Lenin's Moscow Business Conditions Institute beginning in 1920.

Using a composite of economic statistics from France, Germany, Great Britain, and the United States, Kondratieff established the periodic occurrence of a series of several decade-long economic cycles in his 1926 treatise *Die langen Wellen der Konjunktur.* Termed the Kondratieff wave, or K-wave for short, the pattern illustrated cyclical peaks and valleys approximately every 50 years with alternating 25-year up and 25-year down segments. (See Figure 1-1 Kondratieff Wave Business Cycle.)

Tracing the K-wave pattern from the 18th century, you can find the following alternating troughs and peaks: 1720–1740 trough, 1760s peak; 1780–1800 trough, 1810s peak; 1840–1860 trough, 1860s peak; 1880–1900 trough, 1920s peak; 1940–1960 trough and 1970s peak.

Even though Kondratieff published his findings in the twenties, his wave theory successfully called the 1930's Great Depression and

### Figure 1-1
### Kondratieff Wave Business Cycle

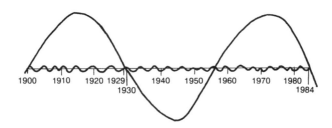

the 1982 economic recession in the United States. Likewise, the stock market followed suit with crashes in both 1937 and 1987, fifty years apart. However, the strong economic performance in the United States during the 1970s didn't hold true to form.

While the K-wave traces a 50-year economic cycle, shorter economic cycles have also gained avid followers over the years. Among the more prominent are a nearly decade-long cycle popularized by a Frenchman, Clemant Juglar, in 1860; a 10-year economic cycle documented by Dutchman J. van Gelderan in 1913; and a 15-to-25-year cycle established by Kuznets.

### Sunspot Phenomena

Current Sunspot theory holds that heightened sunspot activity precedes a bear market. As irrational as linking sun spot activity to stock market action may at first appear, the original Sunspot Indicator did derive from actual economic events.

Sunspot activity peaks in approximate 11-year cycles. Research by 19th century astronomer, Sir William Herschel, correlated changes in the price of wheat with sunspot activity. Herschel discovered that sunspot activity affected the world's climate. Specifically, a peak in sunspot activity coincided with abundant wheat yields, driving prices down. On the other hand, a lull in sunspot activity coincided with poor crop yields and sharply higher wheat prices.

### Modern Economic Cycles

In modern times, governments attempt to influence the length of business cycles through economic policies, such as interest rates, availability of money, trade restrictions and pacts, etc. In addition, factors often not under the direct control of politicians, such as the rate of inflation, unemployment levels, corporate capital spending and the rate of consumer savings, come to bear on the length and severity of many business cycles.

### Index of Leading Economic Indicators

Many business cycle watchers keep a close eye on the Commerce Department's Composite Index of Leading Economic Indicators in order to anticipate changes in economic activity and direction and to make the appropriate investment decision in light of those changes. (See Figure 1-2 Leading Indicators.)

The eleven components of the government's leading indicator index are as follows:

◆ Average workweek of manufacturing production workers

◆ Average weekly initial unemployment claims

◆ New orders for consumer goods and materials

◆ Standard and Poor's S & P 500 index

◆ Orders for plant and equipment

◆ Index of new private housing units

**Figure 1-2**
**Leading Indicators**

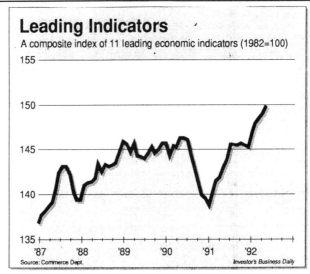

**Leading Indicators**
A composite index of 11 leading economic indicators (1982=100)

Source: Commerce Dept.                                    Investor's Business Daily

**WEAK RECOVERY:** The index of leading economic indicators, the government's main barometer of future economic activity, rose a modest 0.6% in May, notching its fifth-straight monthly gain. However, the increase was less than half the average growth after the 1981-82 recession.

*Source: Investor's Business Daily*

4

◆ Change in manufacturers' unfilled durable goods orders

◆ Change in sensitive commodity prices, excluding foods, feeds, and fibers

◆ Vendor performance

◆ Index of consumer expectations

◆ Money supply (M2)

The index of leading economic indicators is said to be the best single gauge of which direction the economy is headed in the next six to nine months. While no single month can provide an accurate prediction, the trend of the index over several months' time can signal the general trend of the economy.

In conjunction with the index of leading economic indicators, investors also use the coinciding and lagging indicators indexes to help confirm the direction of the economy. For example, coinciding indicators, such as the Federal Reserve Board's index of industrial production and the report on personal income, tend to move hand-in-hand with the economy. Likewise, lagging indicators, such as the average prime rate charged by banks and ratio of consumer debt to personal income, typically trail the economy.

### The Bragg Economic Series Theory

In an effort to develop a trading strategy, not to pick individual securities but to construct the proper portfolio mixture (stocks, long-term bonds, Treasury bills, etc.), Bragg's "Theory of the Economic Series" attempts to redefine the behavior of the economic cycle.

In his book, *Protecting Against Inflation and Maximizing Yield* (Georgia State University Business Publishing Division, 1986), Bragg discusses the failure of mathematical or scientific methods to accurately predict business cycle movements and changes of direction. In their place, Bragg recommends a series of economic periods or cycles characterized not by economic indicators but instead by underlying moods or mass psychology.

He explains four economic periods by the degree of optimism or pessimism and changes in the relationship between optimism and pessimism. The optimism and pessimism refer not only to business conditions and financial markets but also to a general underlying mood as derived from political activities, world events, public attitudes toward leaders, and even from motion pictures and television productions.

Bragg separated his economic series into four periods: Period A, with prevailing pessimism, Period B, with optimism gaining over pessimism, Period C, with optimism prevailing, and Period D, with pessimism gaining over optimism.

Using research covering 75 economic periods and 18 complete economic series, Bragg studied the performance of different investment asset forms and compared their performance from period to period. He concluded that study of his economic series theory can be an effective aid in making trading strategy decisions.

The five-year time frame from 1974 through 1978 constituted a complete economic series with all four mood periods A, B, C, and D. Table 1-1 illustrates Bragg's Theory of the Economic Series.

The average economic series extends approximately 5 years with the shortest being only 2.5 years (1893–95 and 1910–12), while the longest extended 10 years (1920–29). Period A averages about 1 1/3 years, Period B averages one year, Period C averages 1.8 years and, Period D averages .9 of a year.

An understanding of how the cycles work—their reactions to economic, political, and mood-related events and how they in turn impact the investment markets and specific investment asset forms or types—puts the investor in good position to apply various individual prediction systems and to capitalize on the ability to forecast market and stock moves.

### Panics and Crashes

Part and parcel of economic cycles throughout history are a long list of panics and crashes that have provided savvy, patient, and disciplined investors with opportunities for significant investment gains.

## Table 1-1
## Economic Period Characteristics and Asset Form Performance
## 1974-1978

### Period A

Pessimism prevails.

General mood that "poor times" will continue. Standard of living declines.

GNP growth low (.8%).

Modest money supply growth (4%).

Real interest rates negative (-2.5%).

Three-month bill yields up 14% from preceding Period D.

Long-term bonds deliver worst performance, with total yield near zero.

Common stocks very poor performance with negative total yield averaging -4.25%.

Overall, three-month bills give optimum performance 62% of time versus 21% of the time for common stocks and 17% of the time for long-term bonds.

### Period B

Optimism gains over pessimism.

Low inflation, down as much as 70% from preceding Period A.

Real GNP turns negative.

Modest money supply growth (4.1%).

Real interest rates high (10.81%).

Three-month bill yields down 14% from preceding Period A.

Long-term bonds turn in best performance, with total yield of 9.35%.

Common stocks very good performance with total yield of 15.18%.

Overall, long-term bonds gave the optimum yield 47% of the time versus 45% of the time for common stocks and 8% of the time for three-month bills.

### Period C

Optimism prevails.

Standard of living grows at highest rate (4.9%).
General mood that "good times" are here to stay.

Low inflation, similar to preceding Period B.

Real GNP growth unusually high (7%), in contrast to poor performance in preceding Period B.

### Period D

Pessimism gains over optimism.

Standard of living continues to increase (3.10%), but rate not as good as in preceding Period C.

Inflation heats up, nearly double of preceding Period C.

Real GNP growth continues high (5.3%) but lower than in preceding Period C.

*Table continues*

## Table 1-1
## Continued

| Period C | Period D |
|---|---|
| Money supply growth very high (8.1%). | Money supply growth continues high (7.4%). |
| Real interest rates extremely high (14.89%). | Real interest rates drop dramatically to 1.54%. |
| Three-month bill yields lowest for any period, down 28% from preceding Period B and down 38% from Period A. | Three-month bill yields increased 41% from preceding Period C; however, no reverse yield curve yet. |
| Long-term bonds deliver fair return (5.08%) but not as good as preceding Period B. | Long-term bonds deliver poor performance, with total yield of 2.52%. |
| Common stocks' finest performance, with total yield of 18.64%. | Common stocks' lackluster performance, with total yield of 6.55%. |
| Overall, common stocks give the optimum performance 88% of the time versus 12% of the time for long-term bonds. | Overall, common stocks gave the optimum yield 47% of the time versus 32% of the time three-month bills and 21% of the time for long-term bonds. |

Investment writer Harry D. Schultz explained how to survive the next crash and make money as others are heading for the hills in his book *Panics & Crashes and How You Can Make Money Out of Them* (Arlington House, 1972).

Major elements of Schultz's survival strategy for the next crash include having plenty of liquidity (from 50 to 75 percent of your assets in cash or near cash), paying off your home mortgage, shedding your stock holdings and mutual fund holdings, and taking short positions if you are confident a panic is en route. On the hedge side, purchase only federal government and AAA rated corporate bonds and gold, or the shares of mining companies with high-grade gold mines and plenty of reserves.

As in any investment scenario, Schultz maintained that diversification is key in order to spread your risks. In addition, in-depth knowledge of your investment options is critical to success. For example, you could be in the right hedge—gold coins—and still lose money if you don't know which year coins are likely to maintain and even increase the premium they command in the market. Similarly, make sure your liquid assets are safely invested and not in some high-flying savings and loan. Schultz also advises against leaving cash balances with brokerage houses which can also go under in the wake of a crash.

Paramount in Schultz's panic and crash survival strategy is to develop a mindset that allows you to keep your head while all about you are ... panicked. According to Schultz, their rash actions will create ample opportunities for you to purchase investments at a substantial discount to value and their eventual re-bounded prices. All this assumes you had the foresight to build up your liquid assets in order to capitalize on the general panic and irrational investment behavior as others flee the markets.

Panics represent the economy's way of correcting previous excesses. After each panic or crash, the economy or market once again resumed its upward climb after the excesses had been wrung out. While this procedure may take years and even decades in some instances, it has never failed to eventually recover and reach new highs.

Table 1-2 lists some of the more significant panics and crashes in our nation's history.

Learning Schultz's panic and crash survival techniques promises to help you understand the classic warning signs and prepare you to position yourself to avoid the debacle and profit, while other investors see the value of their portfolio holdings plunge.

## TIME CYCLES

Time cycles occur much more frequently such as weekly and monthly time frames. Many investors use technical analysis charting techniques to uncover time cycle patterns that purport to predict

**Table 1–2**
**U.S. Panics and Crashes**

| CRASH | PREVIOUS CONDITIONS |
| --- | --- |
| Panic of 1857 | Vast railroad speculation in wake of California gold rush. |
| Panic of 1901 | Rife speculation in stock market during wild bull market, cornering of Northern Pacific Railroad, wiping out numerous short sellers and margin traders. |
| Panic of 1921 | Postwar boom fueled by U. S. government loans to Allies collapses. |
| Panic of 1929 | Stock market speculation permeated all levels of society. |
| Panic of 1962 | Loss of gold on large scale due to trade imbalance. Also impacted by buildup of inventories in anticipation of 1959 steel strike. |
| Crash of 1987 | Influence of programmed trading and overspeculation. |
| Crash of 1990 | Stalled economic recovery, fears of possible slide back into recession. |

future stock price moves. In general, there is no direct connection between time cycles and overall economic conditions.

### The Elliott Wave

Ralph N. Elliott compiled one of the most extensive and widely followed time cycle theories, the Elliott Wave Principle, in 1939 and beyond. In essence, Elliott determined that bull and bear markets were governed by natural law and exhibited consistent and recognizable cyclical waves patterns which repeated over time.

As theorized by Elliott and his followers, investors could count the waves and predict the next market turn and reap substantial profits.

To greatly simplify the intricate technical premises supporting the Elliott Wave Principle, the theory basically states that market action consists of an uptrend with a series of five waves (three up-waves and two corrective down-waves) followed by a market down-trend with three waves (two down-waves and one up-wave).

Proponents of the theory insist that it's important to pay strict attention to confirmed waves and reversal points. In other words, you must have confirmation that one complete cycle has been completed and another started. Investors who restart their cycle monitoring and investment decisions after only three or four waves on the upside and after one or two waves on the downside leave themselves open to faulty signals and erroneous investment timing decisions.

The biggest criticism of the Elliott Wave Principle is that it does not lend itself to easy interpretation. For example, the irregularity in wave lengths, with one leg extending for only a week or two while another can last months, lends itself to confusion and misinterpretation. Is the trendline a part of a major downleg or merely a pullback in an ongoing uptrend?

With this in mind, David H. Weis in *Trading with the Elliott Wave Principle: A Practical Guide* (Tape Readers Press, 1988) offered a number of wave counting guidelines including the following:

◆ Wave three should not be the shortest in an impulse

◆ Wave four of one degree should not overlap with wave one of the same degree

◆ Wave two cannot bottom below the beginning of wave one of the same degree

◆ Make wave counts that contain alternation between corrective waves of the same degree

◆ Extensions often occur in wave three, which makes it the impulse of greatest gain and acceleration

◆ In wave five, watch for a diagonal triangle in which waves one and four overlap

◆ Never rule out the possibility of a fifth wave failure

◆ Triangles can occur in fourth waves

◆ Remember that wave counts usually have to be adjusted as a move unfolds

Obviously, you won't pick up the Elliott Wave intricacies with one read of the theory, but plenty of investors stand by its usefulness. (See Figure 1-3 Elliott Wave.)

### The Fibonacci Connection

Elliott's development of the Elliott Wave Principle originated from his research into repetitive cycles or series in natural systems. This led Elliott to the research findings of a thirteenth century Italian mathematician, Leonardo Fibonacci.

Fibonacci discovered that a specific number series, in which each number in the series equals the sum of the two numbers preced-

**Figure 1-3**
**Elliott Wave**

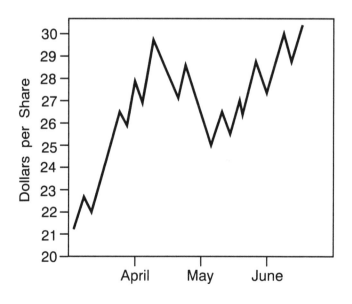

ing it (1,1,2,3,5,8,13,21,34,55,89,144) occurred frequently in nature. For example, the Fibonacci number series accounts for the spirals in sunflower seeds, the arrangement of leaf buds on a stem and the design of a snail's shell.

## Dow Theory

The grandaddy of 'em all, the Dow Theory owes its existence to Charles H. Dow, one of the founders of Dow Jones Company as well as the first editor of the *Wall Street Journal*. Dow theorized in the late 1800s that the trend of overall stock prices could be determined by studying a selected group of stocks. Thus the first market average or index originated, the Dow Jones Industrial Average. (See Figure 1-4 Dow Jones Industrials).

The list of stocks comprising the Dow has changed many times over the years due to mergers and efforts to make the index more representative of the market as well as to take into account stock splits, companies going private and even bankruptcy filings. For example, General Foods dropped from the list after that firm's takeover by Philip Morris. Owens-Illinois was removed when it went private, and Manville fell from the Dow ranks when it filed for bankruptcy protection in the wake of asbestos lawsuits. To make the list more representative, Caterpillar, Disney, and JP Morgan replaced Navistar International, Primerica Corporation and USX in recent years.

In the middle of June, 1992, the following stocks made up the Dow Jones Industrial average:

| *Company* | *Business* |
|---|---|
| Allied Signal | Chemicals, oil & gas, fibers |
| Alcoa | Aluminum |
| American Express | Insurance, investments, travel services |
| AT&T | Telecommunications |
| Bethlehem Steel | Steel |
| Boeing | Aerospace, Aircraft |
| Caterpillar | Heavy duty equipment |
| Chevron | Oil |
| Coca-Cola | Soft drinks |

**Figure 1-4**

**Dow Jones Industrials**

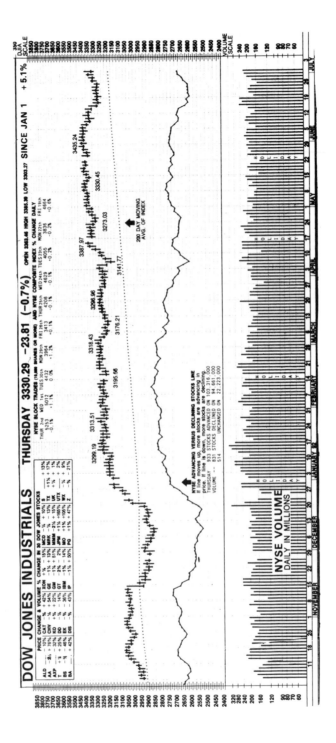

| *Company* | *Business* |
|---|---|
| Disney | Entertainment & amusement parks |
| DuPont | Chemicals, oil & gas |
| Eastman Kodak | Chemicals, photographic |
| Exxon | Oil |
| General Electric | Electrical equipment |
| General Motors | Automotive |
| Goodyear | Tires & rubber |
| IBM | Business machines |
| International Paper | Forest and paper products |
| McDonald's | Fast food & franchising |
| Merck | Pharamaceuticals & specialty chemicals |
| 3M | Tapes & adhesives |
| JP Morgan | Banking |
| Philip Morris | Consumer products |
| Proctor & Gamble | Household & personal care |
| Sears Roebuck | Retail, finance & insurance |
| Texaco | Oil |
| Union Carbide | Chemicals & plastics |
| United Technologies | Aircraft engines |
| Westinghouse | Electrical equipment |
| F.W. Woolworth | Variety & discount retail |

While the Dow garners the largest attention from stock market watchers, its ability to mirror the overall market suffers due to several factors. First of all, since it is a price-weighted average, stocks with a higher market price get more weight. Therefore, it does not represent a true measure of the return of the 30 stocks making up the Dow.

Second, as a composite of giant industrial and service companies, the Dow excludes representation of the thousands of smaller companies traded on the New York Stock Exchange. As a result, the Dow Jones Industrial Average and broader indexes such as the New York Stock Exchange Composite can indicate movement in different directions at the same time.

Over the years, a bevy of other indexes have gained their share of recognition and followers for their representation of different segments of the market. As a result of the dissatisfaction with the Dow Jones Industrial Average, in 1966 the New York Stock Exchange launched the New York Stock Exchange Composite, which traces the action of all stocks listed on the Big Board.

Among other major indexes monitored by market watchers, the American Market Value Index tracks the performance of 800 American Stock Exchange companies (See Figure 1-5 American Stock Exchange), the NASDAQ Composite measures the performance of 3,500-plus over-the-counter stocks traded via the automated quotations system of the National Association of Securities Dealers (See Figure 1-6 NASDAQ Composite), the Value Line Composite follows the action of some 1,700 stocks across the broad spectrum of the NYSE, AMEX, and OTC markets while the broadest index, the Wilshire 5000 Equity Index, represents a composite of all NYSE, AMEX, and OTC issues.

The Standard & Poor's 500 index represents 400 industrial, 40 financial, 40 utility, and 20 transportation companies and also serves as a benchmark index for other indexes and the performance of many mutual funds. (See Figure 1-7 Mutual Fund Index).

No matter which market index you place your faith in, knowledge of the Dow Theory promises to help to put market moves into perspective.

While others have later further expounded on and tried to refine the Dow Theory, the original theory created by Charles Dow with the aid of S. A. Nelson, both editors of *The Wall Street Journal*, was developed as a method to track changes in stock prices and became popularized as a way to forecast changes in business conditions.

The Dow Theory rested on the concept that market movements consisted of three segments: a primary movement, a secondary movement, and the daily movement, all of which operated simultaneously. According to Dow and Nelson, the primary movement can last up to four years and represents the major bull or bear market. The secondary trend can last from several weeks to several months and reflects a steep retraction in a bull market or a strong rise in a bear market. Finally, the daily movements show short-term price fluctuations with the primary and secondary trends.

### Figure 1-5
### American Stock Exchange

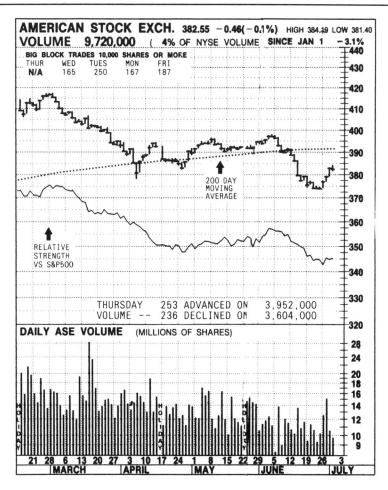

Source: Investor's Business Daily

During the course of a major primary move, there can be any number of secondary movements. Since the primary movement pur-

## Figure 1-6
## NASDAQ Composite

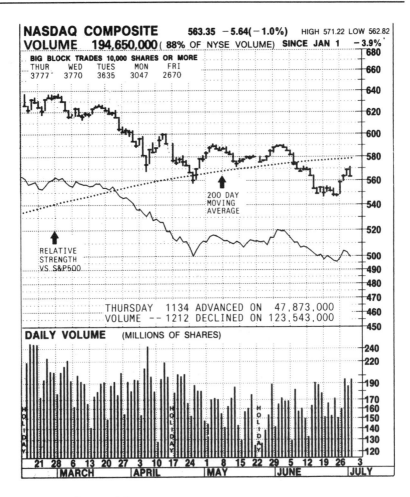

Source: Investor's Business Daily

ports to signal the future direction of the economy and the stock market, it ranks first in importance, followed by the secondary move-

**Figure 1-7**
**Mutual Fund Index**

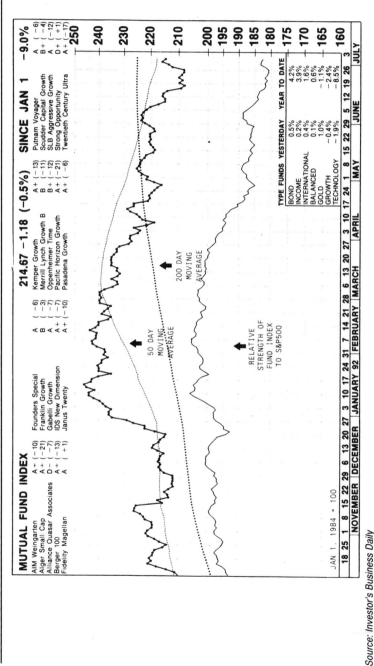

Source: *Investor's Business Daily*

ment. Daily stock price movements are considered unimportant in prediction of the market's direction except that they help determine the slope of the secondary and primary trend lines.

A bull market is regarded as ongoing as long as each successive advance of the primary trend peaks higher than the one preceding it. Likewise, a bear market is defined as one in which each successive decline carries the market to new lows. (See Figure 1-8 Dow Primary Uptrend and Figure 1-9 Dow Primary Downtrend.)

Should a rally movement fail to penetrate the previous high and then the market declines to fall below a previous low, the primary movement has switched from a major uptrend to a major downtrend. (See Figure 1-10 Dow Theory Bear Market Signal.)

Dow Theory requires a corroboration by both the Dow Jones Industrial Average and the Dow Transportation Average for official confirmation of a major market direction change.

**Figure 1-8**
**Dow Primary Uptrend**

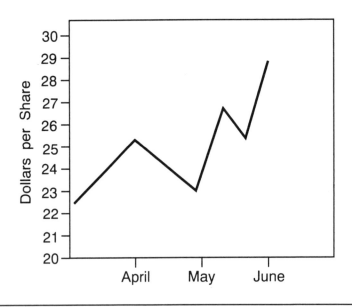

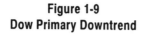

**Figure 1-9**
**Dow Primary Downtrend**

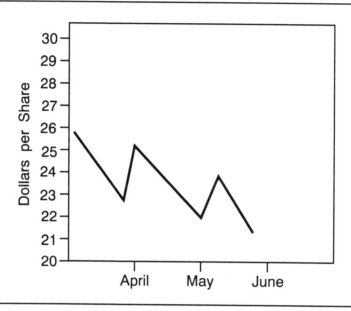

## Touhey Bull Market Buying System

In his book, *Stock Market Forecasting for Alert Investors* (AMACOM, 1980), John C. Touhey expounded on three buying selection investment principles designed to enable investors to purchase stocks that consistently advance farther than the market averages during major bull swings.

*Buying Principle I:* Bear Market Declines. Touhey speculated that the stocks with the largest price declines in the previous bear market offered the best opportunities for the largest advances in the next bull market. Several factors contributed to this analysis. First of all, the stocks with the largest declines in the previous bear market probably exhibited more volatility than the average stock. Therefore, it was reasonable to expect that they would also be more volatile on the upswing.

**Figure 1-10**
**Dow Theory Bear Market Signal**

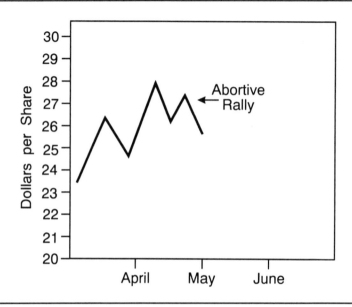

Second, overpessimism during the bear market meant many stocks ended up seriously undervalued at the end of the bear market even though their fundamentals had not deteriorated. Therefore, as more reasonable valuations take place, these stocks should beat the market averages during the next bull market.

Using a sample of 100 stocks, Touhey calculated the bull market advance for the 16 stocks which had declined more than 75 percent in the previous bear market. During the 1975–1976 bull market, the 16 stocks gained an average advance of 159 percent versus only 108 percent for the 100 stocks as a whole.

*Buying Principle 2:* Small Market Capitalization. Since it takes less money to move stocks with smaller capitalization, Touhey theorized that small cap stocks have the potential to move farthest in bull markets. Testing his hypothesis, Touhey calculated the returns for 15 low cap stocks versus a universe of 100 stocks from the bear market low in October 1974 to the bull market high in January 1977. The results: the small cap stocks earned an average return of 175 percent versus only 108 percent for the 100 stocks overall.

*Buying Principle 3:* Selling Price Lower than Quick Assets. This principle consists of using the relationship between quick assets (short-term assets less both long-term and short-term liabilities) divided by the number of outstanding shares and market price per share.

According to Touhey, a select number of companies will be trading at a market share price less than the quick asset per share valuation. This indicates an undervalued situation and the stocks in these companies should be purchased when the market indicators signal a major bull market swing.

Using the same stock universe discussed in Principle 2, Touhey discovered that the 14 stocks selling at less than their quick asset per share valuation gained an average 211 percent versus the 108 percent average gain for the whole 100 company sample.

### Touhey Bear Market Selling System

As important as developing a well-thought out stock purchasing system, Touhey also realized that unless you unload your stocks at the opportune time, you run the risk of reducing your investment gains and even subjecting your investment portfolio to unnecessary losses. In order to prevent that from happening, he developed a series of selling principles.

*Selling Principle 1:* Price/Earnings Ratio. Touhey uses the price/earnings ratio as a forecaster of how far a stock will decline in a bear market. Simply put, the higher a stock's P/E ratio, the greater percentage of its price it will suffer in a decline. In light of this, Touhey recommends selling or shorting those stocks with the highest P/E ratios.

*Selling Principle 2.* Low Dividend Yields. Since higher dividend yields help support a stock's price in the face of market declines, Touhey suggests selling or shorting stocks with the lowest dividend yields in the face of a bear market.

*Selling Principle 3:* Previous Bull Market Advance. As the opposite of Buying Principle 1, this selling principle advises selling or selling short the stocks which have advanced the most in the previous bull market.

As with the buying principles, Touhey performed market research with his selling principles that helped support his conclusions. For example: Declines for the 15 stocks with the highest P/E ratios averaged 68 percent versus an average 53 percent decline for the 100 stock universe during the 1973–1974 bear market; the 21 stocks with dividend yields below 1 percent posted an average decline of 65 percent compared with the average 53 percent decline; and the 14 stocks which tripled during the previous bull market declined an average 70 percent from the bull market high in January 1973 to the bear market low in October 1974 versus a drop of an average 53 percent for the universe sample.

### Stoken Investment Timing System

Dick A. Stoken analyzed over sixty years of investment history to come up with the prediction system in his book *Strategic Investment Timing* (Probus Publishing, 1990). According to Stoken, four fundamental indicators combine into a model that has accurately pinpointed every important turn in investment markets. Not only does Stoken's theory purport to call the turns, it also signals when to switch from stocks to alternative investments such as gold, real estate or commodities, etc. (See Figure 1-11 Stock Market and Gold Chart.) Over the 63-year period under study, the indicators sent out the correct signal at the start of each and every bull and bear market within an average 6 percent of the exact high or low.

The single most important factor impacting the economy and investment markets is the investment climate. Key to the investment climate, the level and direction of interest rates signals whether or not a turn in the economy and stock market is in the cards.

Interest rate warning signs include a drop in the 90-Day T-Bill rate to its lowest level in fifteen months and when AAA corporate bond rates hit a fifteen-month low. The occurrence of either of those

**Figure 1-11**
**Stock Market and Gold: 1971–1983**

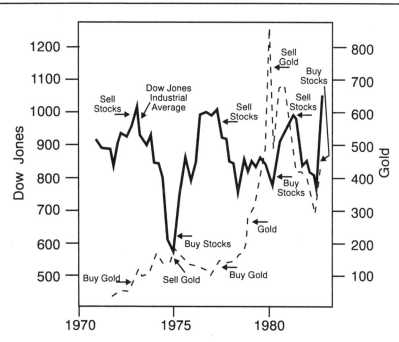

*Source:* Dick A. Stoken, *Strategic Investment Timing,* Probus Publishing Company, 1990

two events triggers a powerful expansionary force that promises to send both the economy and stock market soaring.

On the other extreme, the appearance of seven-year highs for both the 90-Day T-Bill rate and the AAA corporate rate represents a shot across the bow for a plunging economy and stock market in the days and months ahead.

Another important influence on the investment climate comes from the political arena. The presidential election cycle translates into a 15-month favorable phase beginning in early October, two years prior to the presidential election, and lasting through early January of the election year.

According to Stoken's research, this 15-month period has generated an average gain of 25 percent for the Dow Jones Industrial Average since 1932 versus an average gain of only 1 percent for the remaining 33-months of the political cycle. (See Figure 1-12 Political Cycles: 15-Month Favorable Phase.) Even more interesting, not one single recession originated during this 15-month favorable time frame. A further discussion of presidential elections and the stock market appears later in this chapter.

### Figure 1-12
### Political Cycles: 15-Month Favorable Phase

| October 1 | Dow | January 2 | Dow | Gain (%) | Gain/Loss During Remaining 33 Months |
|---|---|---|---|---|---|
| 1934 | 90 | 1936 | 144 | 60 | (1) |
| 1938 | 143 | 1940 | 151 | 6 | (28) |
| 1942 | 109 | 1944 | 131 | 24 | 30 |
| 1946 | 171 | 1948 | 181 | 6 | 26 |
| 1950 | 228 | 1952 | 269 | 18 | 33 |
| 1954 | 359 | 1956 | 485 | 35 | 9 |
| 1958 | 530 | 1960 | 679 | 28 | (16) |
| 1962 | 571 | 1964 | 766 | 34 | (1) |
| 1966 | 757 | 1968 | 906 | 20 | (16) |
| 1970 | 760 | 1972 | 889 | 18 | (32) |
| 1974 | 604 | 1976 | 858 | 42 | (2) |
| 1978 | 871 | 1980 | 824 | (5) | 10 |
| 1982 | 907 | 1984 | 1252 | 38 | 8 |
| 1986* | | | | | |
| | | Average Gain | | 25% | 2% |

Note: Negative numbers are indicated by parentheses.
* No favorable phase because it did not have a prior slump.

Source: Dick A. Stoken, *Strategic Investment Timing*, Probus Publishing Company, 1990

Under the presidential election scenario, the level of interest rates can be ignored since the investment climate turns favorable regardless of their level during this phase of the political cycle.

The third factor, inflation, can cause an otherwise favorable investment climate to prove disastrous for stock investments and a fertile ground for real assets such as gold, commodities, real estate, and collectibles.

For keeping tabs on this valuable indicator, Stoken suggests monitoring the Producers Price Index compiled by the Bureau of Labor Statistics. An inflationary spiral starts when a price increase reaches 5 percent or more and is at its highest reading in a year. However, Stoken cautions that the rate of inflation must also be gathering momentum and that people start believing in the inflationary spiral and begin to change their spending and saving habits.

On the deflation side of the coin, a one-year low in the Producer's Price Index sends a clear signal of deflation taking place. Typically, another inflationary bout doesn't occur until two years after a deflationary period has terminated.

An inflationary spiral will stop stock market progress while it makes real assets more attractive. In the three periods of runaway inflation since the end of World War II, purchasing power loss averaged 25 percent. On the other hand, had investors followed the inflation signals and converted to gold investments, they would have earned a return of 145 percent during 1972 through 1974 and 405 percent between 1977 and 1980.

According to Stoken, investors following the inflation indicators would have participated and profited in every hyper-inflationary period, plus they would have been fully invested during the bulk of the post World War II bull markets.

Finally, the psychology of investors impacts the stock markets, creating periods of pessimism when stock prices are cheap in relation to value and periods of optimism when stock prices become expensive in relation to value. Stoken's research shows that no sustained bull market has begun until the Dow had fallen into a two-year low. Accordingly, the best time to purchase stocks is one week after the market hits its two-year low point.

This "buy zone" continues until nine months have passed since the Dow made a two-year high. The stock market is then in a "caution zone" which lasts until the Dow once again drops to a two-year low, restarting the cycle. When the Dow hits a five-year low, extreme pessimism has taken over the market, creating a stock buying opportunity five months after experiencing that low point.

Stoken contends that using the above indicators, an investor can design a flexible investment timing strategy that deftly moves him or her out of stocks or real assets in tune with the investment climate and inflationary and deflationary signals.

## The Presidential Cycle

The most widely recognized time cycle investment prediction system in the United States stretches back more than a century and a half to the presidency of Andrew Jackson, In fact, the cycle itself ties stock market performance to the presidential election cycle.

According to Yale Hirsch, editor of the 1992, 25th edition of *The Stock Trader's Almanac*, the last two years (election year and pre-election year) of the 41 administrations since 1832 produced a total net market gain of 527 percent, significantly outperforming the 74 percent advance during the first two years of those same administrations.

In recent history, the four-year cycle beginning in 1984 reversed course with the pre-election year dropping 3 percent, the election year delivering flat returns, and the post-election year and mid-term year posting strong gains of 20 percent or more.

Over the past 12 presidential elections, the stock market, as measured by the Standard & Poor's 500 Index, rose 12 times, or 83 percent, during the election year versus only two declines. In comparison, non-election years have only posted a gain 65 percent of the time.

The two declines came on the heels of Democratic presidents being elected to the nation's highest office. The first occurred in 1948 with Truman's election and the market's decline of 0.7 percent. Next, John Kennedy gained admission to the White House, and the market dropped 3.0 percent. However, the market rose after Lyndon

Johnson's election by 13.0 percent in 1964, and climbed again in 1976 by 19.1 percent as Democrat Jimmy Carter won our nation's highest office. (See Table 1-3.)

A number of theories exist purporting to explain the behavior of stock prices within the election-year cycle. Whether you subscribe to the theory that political campaign activity spurs the market or that actions taken by those currently in control of the White House to spur the economy and win votes flows over into stock market prices, it's clear that the election year cycle has indeed impacted market performance, at least from a historical perspective.

### Table 1–3
### Stocks Gains in Presidential Election Years

| Election Year | President | Party | S & P 500 Change |
|---|---|---|---|
| 1948 | Truman | Democrat | -0.7% |
| 1952 | Eisenhower | Republican | +11.8% |
| 1956 | Eisenhower | Republican | +2.6% |
| 1960 | Kennedy | Democrat | -3.0% |
| 1964 | Johnson | Democrat | +13.0% |
| 1968 | Nixon | Republican | +7.7% |
| 1972 | Nixon | Republican | +15.6% |
| 1976 | Carter | Democrat | +19.1% |
| 1980 | Reagan | Republican | +25.8% |
| 1984 | Reagan | Republican | +1.4% |
| 1988 | Bush | Republican | +12.4% |
| 1992 | Clinton | Democrat | +7.7% |

# 2

# Technical Predictors

## TECHNICAL ANALYSIS

Just as investors seek to refine their investment strategy and boost portfolio returns via application of the Dow Theory (with its ability to forecast future economic and market trends though primary and secondary movements in stock market prices), followers of other forms of technical analysis rely on the interpretation of a myriad of chart patterns and calculations of various averages to point their way to extraordinary investment profits.

Strictly speaking, technical analysis refers to the study of stock market action both in the aggregate and for individual securities. Technical analysts place heavy emphasis on charting techniques as well as averages in predicting the future course of the overall market and the price of specific stocks. They utilize price and volume trends in establishing their purchase and selling points, ranges and strategies.

The main thrust lies in isolating price and volume movements believed to signal the direction of market and stock prices. The use of charts helps decipher the complex relationships hidden in stock market and security performance numbers. According to technical analysis theory, the charts graphically display and highlight certain trends, relationships, and patterns.

Avid "techies" study the trendlines, formations, averages, gaps, resistance and support levels, and reversals in order to decipher the code of trading profits.

Chart monitoring is based on the premise that history will repeat itself in patterned movements which can be identified in advance based on previous price behavior. Analysis of past market and stock actions, as illustrated by charts, helps to predict the investment future. In theory, if the stock market or a particular stock is strong or weak, a properly constructed chart will reflect that situation.

Chart patterns appear endless with head and shoulders, double tops and double bottoms, ascending tops, reversals, saucers, breakouts, support and resistance levels, and consolidation formations representing some of the more familiar types.

Without a doubt, market and stock prices move in trends, at least until influencing factors alter the demand and supply relationship, which contributes to how much investors are willing to pay for a given security. Whether those factors relate to investment fundamentals such as asset values or earnings or technical price patterns, each investor must decipher for him-or herself.

Before looking at specific technical predictors, a brief discussion of fundamental analysis is in order.

## FUNDAMENTAL ANALYSIS

In contrast to technical analysis, fundamental analysis disregards the purely technical approach to patterns, averages, and charting and concentrates on analyzing and uncovering the company's intrinsic value through a review of the firm's financial statements, its operating and financial performance, and the comparison of the firm with other industry companies or another stock universe.

While technical analysts pore over charts, prices, volume relationships, and trendlines, the fundamental analyst's stock-in-trade consists of studying asset valuation, revenues and earnings performance, company products, advanced technology, niche markets, market barriers, competition, marketing thrusts, profit margins, dividend policy, research and development expenditures, labor relations, acquisition and divestiture opportunities, and the quality of top management.

In other words, the fundamental analyst attempts to decipher the company's particular strengths and weaknesses and assess how they will impact the firm's future operating and financial performance and, ultimately, the direction and strength of the firm's stock price movements. In addition, the fundamental analyst factors in the projected effects of market conditions, economic forecasts, interest rate trends, government regulation, inflation rates, the political climate, environmental concerns and other outside forces.

Popular methods used to help uncover a firm's intrinsic value, and thus what price the market should value the firm at once its true worth becomes known by the overall market, include price/earnings ratio evaluation, discounted dividend models, and asset valuation. These fundamental analysis predictors and others will be discussed in more detail in Chapter 4, Investment Theories.

The technical analysis bible originated with the 1948 publication of *Technical Analysis of Stock Trends* by John Magee and Robert D. Edwards. Many editions later (the most recent edition released by John Magee Inc. in 1992) this technical analysis treatise still garners much use by avid followers of this investment strategy. It is considered must reading by even the most casual of investors.

While one may not completely agree with every facet of technical analysis, there are enough investors who do believe in its predicting power that it almost becomes self-fulfilling. With that in mind, it's important for every serious investor to be aware of the impact of technical analysis on stock market behavior and to possess at least a rudimentary knowledge of technical analysis and its major trends and patterns.

## Point and Figure Method

Attributed to Charles Dow, point and figure charts track the stock price movements using X's (for price increases) and O's (for price declines). Each mark is placed in a vertical column until a change in price direction or reversal takes place; then a new column is started to indicate a new trend. (See Figure 2-1 Point and Figure Chart.)

Instead of a trendline, the resulting pattern of X's and O's reflect a stock's price action and ability to sustain an upward or downward price movement.

In contrast to bar charts, which track prices at specific intervals, point and figure charts only create a new chart mark when the price

**Figure 2-1**
**Point and Figure Chart**

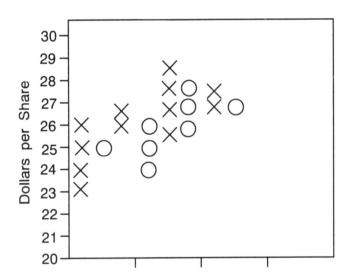

changes by a specific amount. Since closing prices are rounded off to whole numbers, minor fluctuations in prices are ignored. Point and figure charts can be created using even wider price ranges. For example, some charts only record price changes in excess of five or more points on the Dow Jones Industrial Average.

Referring to the Point and Figure Chart in Figure 2-1, closing prices of 25 1/4, 25 1/8 and 25 3/8 on three consecutive days would result in only one mark on the chart, assuming the first price of 25 1/4 moved either upward from the $24 per share level (rounded) or downward from the $26 per share level (rounded) for the previous price change. If the price continues to trade in a narrow range day after day, the point and figure chart would not change during that time. The next mark will be plotted only after the stock "breaks out" of that narrow price range.

Since point and figure charts do not reflect either time or volume, their key price determinant factor is change in price direction. They possess a distinct advantage over bar charts, which cannot indicate price reversals easily. Typically, it takes three marks to confirm a price trend reversal. For example, the O in the second column and the two X's in the third column of Figure 2-1 do not indicate price reversals, while the three O's in column four and the four X's in column five do reflect bona fide price reversals.

As a predictor, point and figure charts are intended to provide guidance in interpreting the future length, height, and duration of these price movements.

Their ability to pinpoint reversals aids in deciphering bullish and bearish signals, while bottom and top formations show support and resistance levels to use in stock purchasing and selling decision making.

Disadvantages of point and figure charts include: the intra-day price fluctuations can't be shown, the use of whole numbers may result in investors missing important price shifts, and the lack of a volume gauge can give the same weight to thinly traded price moves as to major volume-related price changes.

As with other charting methods, trendlines can be added to point and figure charts to highlight the direction of the dominant price trend. (See Figure 2-2 Point and Figure Chart With Trendlines.)

### Bar Charts

The other major charting method consists of constructing bars or lines to indicate price movements. A vertical bar shows the high and low price range during a specified time frame. Opening prices are

### Figure 2-2
### Point and Figure Chart with Trendlines

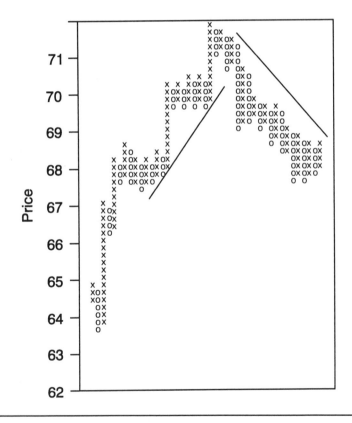

indicated by a small horizontal line extending to the left of the vertical bar, while closing prices are indicated by a small horizontal line extending to the right.

In contrast to point and figure charts, bar charts reflect the price action over time. Depending on the intent of the investor, bar charts can cover time periods from months right down to real time, tracking with sophisticated computer software. (See Figure 2-3 Bar Chart.)

As with point and figure charts, trendlines aid interpretation of long-term market and stock price trends. (See Figure 2-4 Bar Chart With Trendlines.)

Bar charts take prices into account over a time span. While point and figure charts concentrate on price reversals, bar charts show the degree of price action or inaction within a specific time frame. A refinement to the plain vanilla bar chart adds a volume indicator that

**Figure 2-3**
**Bar Chart**

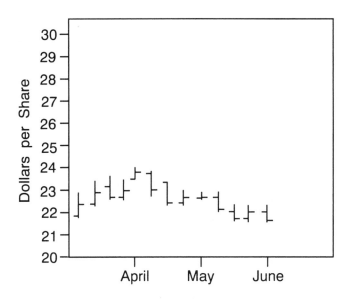

**Figure 2-4**
**Bar Chart with Trendlines**

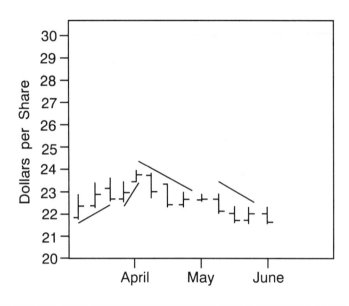

shows the strength or weakness behind a particular price move. (See Figure 2-5 Bar Chart with Volume Indicator.)

### Trendlines and Channels

Using straight lines, you can connect successively higher or lower tops or bottoms, helping you determine which trend remains in force. Typically, primary trends last for periods exceeding several months and often extending for years, while secondary or intermediary trends last from one to three months and minor trends run for a few weeks or less.

Prices move in trends in reaction to the imbalance between demand and supply for the stock. As demand exceeds supply, the

## Figure 2-5
## Bar Chart with Volume Indicator

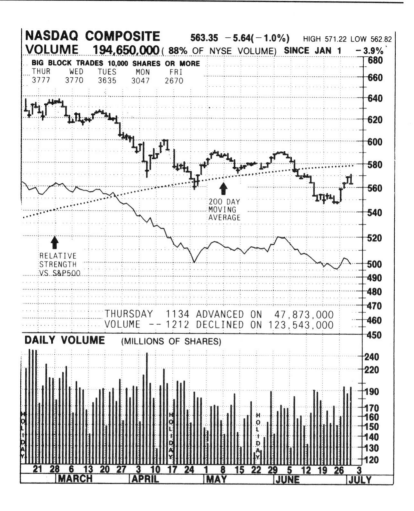

Source: *Investor's Business Daily*

trendline will move upward to the right as investors drive the price higher. Conversely, if supply exceeds demand, the trendline will slope downward to the right, as the excess supply of stock pulls the price lower. Should an equilibrium between supply and demand exist, the stock price will trade sideways in a narrow trading range.

During a rising trend, all prices will stay above the uptrend line, and during a declining trend, all prices will stay below the downtrend line. Once either the uptrend or downtrend line is penetrated, the previous price trend is reversed.

According to strict technical analysis theory, a penetration of an uptrend line signals a sell position, while penetration of a downtrend line should trigger a buying opportunity. Of course, investors take other considerations into play, such as the degree of penetration, volume trends, etc. Also, the slope of the trend line must be evaluated. The steeper the slope of the trend line, the more likely it will be penetrated, sending false buy or sell signals. The existence of a large number of tops and bottoms lends support to the continuation of the ongoing trend. After penetration of a trendline occurs, a new trendline is established, creating a fan-like effect. (See Figure 2-6 Fan Lines.)

At times, stock prices will trade within a range, creating a channel line that runs parallel to the trendline. In a declining market price trend, the channel line will run below the price activity, and in a rising market or price uptrend the channel will run above the price activity. (See Figure 2-7 Channel Line with Downtrend.)

Identification of the trendline and its parallel channel line signals investment-timing opportunities. For example, points 1, 3 and 5 represent selling levels, while points 2 and 4 indicate excellent buying opportunities. Figure 2-7 also illustrates a penetration of the downtrend line at point 6. This breakout, if supported by other technical indicators such as volume, etc., promises a sustained and profitable run on the upside with periodic but limited price retracements.

If you split the channel roughly down the middle, you can establish buying and selling zones since it will be impossible to perfectly time the high and low points. (See Figure 2-8 Channel Investment Zones.)

**Figure 2-6**
**Fan Lines**

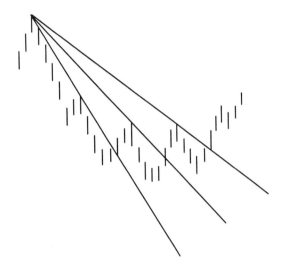

**Figure 2-7**
**Channel Line with Downtrend**

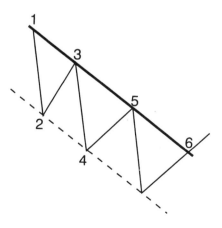

**Figure 2-8**
**Channel Investment Zones**

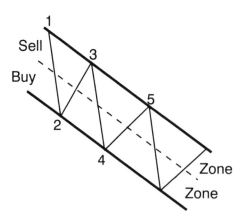

In the situation where stocks trade within a narrow range and don't exhibit any definite trendline direction, technical analysts suggest constructing a bandwidth using the high and low for a period of days. Should the price break above the bandwidth in a forward look, a positive trend movement has been established and vice versa for a downside breakout. If prices break out both above and below the bandwidth, you can construct a trend movement index by subtracting the sum of the positive trend movements over a period of days from the sum of the negative trend movements for the same time period and then dividing this difference by the sum of the positive and negative trend movements. The further the index is from zero, the stronger the trend signal.

Gerald Appel, president of Signalalert Corporation in Great Neck, New York, which publishes *Systems and Forecasts*, presents a bevy of trendline prediction systems in his book, *Winning Market Systems* (Windsor Books, 1989). In addition to a discussion of the bandwidth strategy referenced above, Appel states that it is often possible to predict trendline violations in advance of their occurrence.

The investor who can accomplish this will be able to take long positions at lower prices and sell or short stocks at higher prices than available at the traditional signal point, translating into higher investment gains. The strategy involves monitoring the channel line and the number of times the trendline has been touched in the past.

Stock market movements frequently occur in three waves following the breakout from a base. In other words, major movements consist of three waves in the primary direction, interrupted by two corrective waves. According to Appel, the third reaction to the trendline frequently penetrates it. Penetration can be anticipated if two corrective reactions to the trendline have already taken place.

## Patterned Predictors

The purpose of employing technical analysis chart systems lies in identifying telltale historical price patterns for predicting future market and stock price movements.

In order to successfully trade using chart analysis, the investor must be able to distinguish between consolidation, continuation, and reversal patterns and make the appropriate investment decisions based on that information.

### Head and Shoulders

Perhaps the most recognized chart pattern, the head and shoulders formation represents the classic reversal pattern and is frequently used by pattern watchers to time their purchases and sales. Head and shoulders formations can signal both tops and bottoms. (See Figure 2-9 Head and Shoulders Top and Figure 2-10 Head and Shoulders Bottom.)

The top pattern consists of a final top rally (head) preceded and followed by two lesser, similar but not identical, rallies (shoulders). In contrast, an inverse head and shoulders characterize the bottom pattern. In either case, the formation signals the end of a major trend and a pattern reversal.

In addition to the recognizable pattern, volume plays a crucial role in determining the path an investor should take. According to theory, during head and shoulders tops the heaviest volume occurs

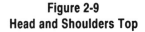

**Figure 2-9**
**Head and Shoulders Top**

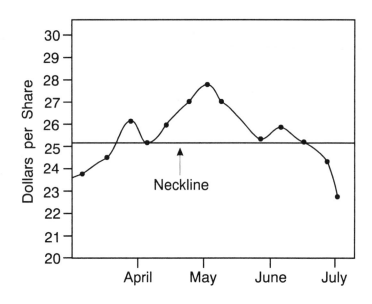

with the formation of the left shoulder and as prices peak out at the head. Formation of the right shoulder typically takes place under significantly lower trading volumes.

After the second shoulder takes form, a neckline can be drawn under the bottoms of the two shoulders. Penetration of this neckline represents the final confirmation of the head and shoulders pattern and signals an opportunity to sell short in advance of the coming bear market. Obviously, other purchase and sale opportunities arise during the creation of other portions of the figure. Penetration of the neckline from the head and shoulders bottom pattern means a break-out for a sustained and strong upswing.

**Figure 2-10**
**Head and Shoulders Bottom**

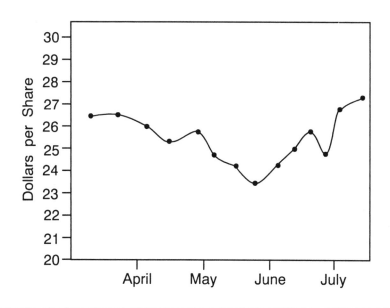

### Double Tops and Double Bottoms

Another popular pattern, the double top and double bottom formations, looks like an 'M' (top) or 'W' (bottom). Technical analysts caution against assuming too early that a double top or double bottom is
in process. If you make your investment decision too soon, you leave
yourself open to significant losses. Confirmation of the formation
occurs only after the valley has been broken or the hill has been
aborted, for the double top and double bottom, respectively. (See
Figure 2-11 Double Top and Figure 2-12 Double Bottom.) These patterns can also transform themselves into triple tops and triple bottoms.

Other common reversal patterns include the rounded bottom or
saucer, rising and falling wedges and reversal day tops and reversal

**Figure 2-11**
**Double Top**

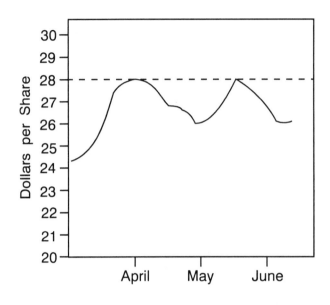

day bottoms. Be careful in distinguishing between the different types of pattern and what each forecasts for the coming market and stock prices. While the term falling wedges conjures up a mental image of 'falling prices', in actuality it signals an upcoming rally. (See Figure 2-13 Falling Wedge.)

### Consolidation Patterns

Moving from reversals to consolidation patterns, we find symmetrical triangles, ascending and descending right angles, flags and pennants, rectangles and gaps. While you can ferret out your own description of most of these patterns and how they are supposed to predict future price activity, a brief discussion of gaps is in order.

**Figure 2-12**
**Double Bottom**

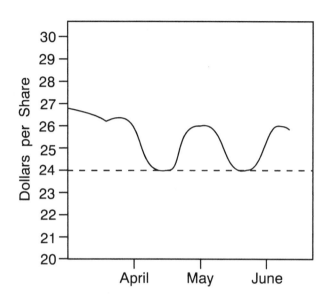

*Gaps*

Gaps represent significant trading information and can be extremely valuable in noticing the beginning of a major move, measuring the extent of a move, or confirming the termination of a trend. Gaps fall into four classifications: common, breakaway, measuring, and runaway and exhaustion.

Gaps occur when the lowest price on one day is higher than the highest price on the preceding day. In other words, there is no overlap of the plotted lines for the trading ranges for two consecutive trading days. (See Figure 2-14 Trading Gap.)

For example, Figure 2-14 illustrates a trading gap between the high price of $25 1/2 per share on one day and the low price of $26 3/4 per share on the following trading day.

**Figure 2-13**
**Falling Wedge**

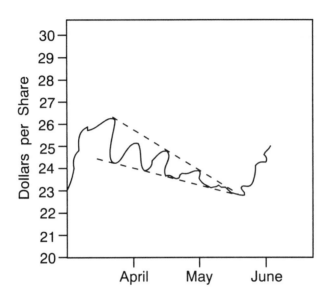

One common misconception is that gaps must be closed prior to major moves away from the gap area. This faulty belief has cost numerous investors lost trading opportunities while they waited for the gap to close.

Common gaps typically form during order imbalances in sideways or consolidation trading situations. They are frequently closed within a short time frame. Most technical analysts attach no significance to common gaps.

Breakaway gaps also take place in connection with consolidation activity. However, they develop at the completion of the consolidation phase with a move that "breaks" away from the pattern with a gap. This break demonstrates strength in the direction of the gap. Accompanied by heavy volume, the breakaway gap forecasts continuation of the move away from the gap area.

**Figure 2-14**
**Trading Gap**

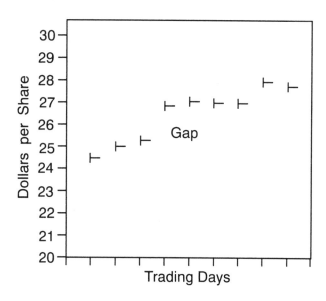

Measuring or runaway gaps form, not in congestion or consolidation areas but along rapid, straightline advance or decline lines, usually near the middle of the price movement. This midpoint reference helps the investor to determine the remaining duration of the runaway movement, hence the terms, *measuring* and *runaway*.

Exhaustion gaps take place at the end of a major, fast-paced move and are considered to mark the end of the move. Confusion between measuring gaps and exhaustion gaps can cause investors to position themselves incorrectly and to miss significant investment gains during the last half of a major move. Volume serves as the major clue to help distinguish between measuring gaps and exhaustion gaps. Typically, particularly heavy trading volume accompanies the arrival of an exhaustion gap.

## Figure 2-15
## Gap Comparison

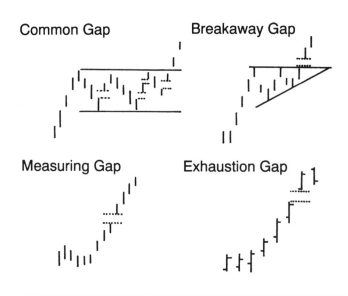

Common Gap

Breakaway Gap

Measuring Gap

Exhaustion Gap

For a visual analysis of the four gap types, review Figure 2-15 Gap Comparison.

### Support and Resistance Predictors

Inherent in many of the chart patterns and technical analysis of price movements, support and resistance levels offer valuable investment information. Support and resistance levels arise as demand and supply equalize and shift the price movement from a rising or descending pattern into a period of consolidation.

Support is the price level at which buyers come in and stabilize the decline, while resistance is the price level where sellers dump their holdings and take their profits. Guidelines for using support and resistance levels for investment opportunities include buying when a stock returns to a support level after a temporary rise, selling when the stock hits and stays at a resistance level, and selling when a stock penetrates a support base.

The more often a stock price reverses from a support or resistance level, the more confidence investors have that the stock will continue to trade within those barriers. After the price finally works to penetrate a support or resistance level, that level often takes on the opposite character. For example, if the price breaks through the resistance level of $27 per share, that $27 per share level then becomes a support level under which the price won't decline. (See Figure 2-16 Support and Resistance Levels.)

In addition to price levels serving as support and resistance levels, trendlines can represent areas of support and resistance that

### Figure 2-16
### Support and Resistance Levels

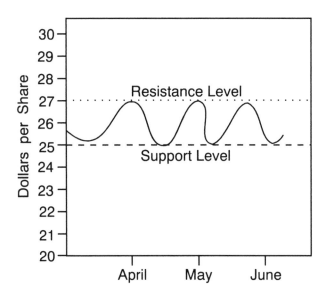

**Figure 2-17**
**Support Trendline**

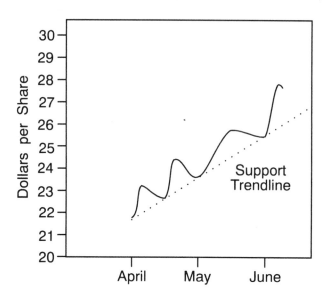

travel across different price levels. (See Figure 2-17 Support Trend-line.)

**Retracement Theory**

To be sure, the market and individual stocks do not move continuously upward or continuously downward. All engage in a period or periods of retracement during which they move in the opposite direction of the major movement.

Each retracement gives back some of the ground captured by the primary move. If a retracement greater than the primary move occurs, it must be considered a reversal of the primary trend.

The retracement theory seeks to establish the predicted length of the retracement itself in order to determine optimum purchase and sale points or ranges.

While no precise retracement measurement has been discovered, most technical analysts subscribe to the 1/3 to 2/3 retracement school of thought.

### Three Peaks and Domed House

One of the more unusual charting patterns owes its initiation into the world of technical analysis to George Lindsay, who presented his findings in *The 1971 Encyclopedia of Stock Market Techniques.*

According to Lindsay, the three peaks and dome house chart pattern looks similar to traditional tops and bottoms, and even encloses both tops and bottoms, but is not a top and bottom formation itself. He counters other technicians who claim that irregular markets do not follow any recognizable pattern and therefore fail to contain any predictive ability.

Lindsay claims his research supports the belief that the so-called haphazard movements of irregular markets have followed the same basic pattern at least 60 percent of the time over the 150 years covered in his research.

Simply stated, the pattern exhibits three peaks followed by a sharp decline (called the separating decline since it separates the three peaks from the next formation). The sharp decline typically consists of at least two selling waves before returning to an upward movement culminating in a domed house. After completion of the domed house, the actions head into a steep and rapid decline, dropping to the level at which it originally began or even lower. (See Figure 2-18 Three Peaks and Domed House.)

The three peaks and domed house pattern worked up through the 1964–1966 period. However, since then a quick perusal of market moves shows a few different twists. It looks like there might be some overlap in the peaks portion of the pattern from one period to another. Taking that into consideration, there appears to be three peaks between 1965–1966 and a domed house in late 1968 followed by a sharp decline into mid–1970.

## Figure 2-18
## Three Peaks and Domed House

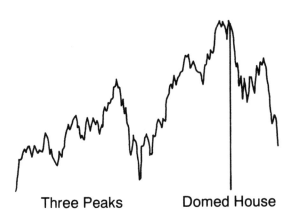

Three Peaks          Domed House

The pattern fits the 1970 rise to a 1972 peak and a sharp decline bottoming out in 1974. From then on, peaks and possible domed houses do occur but the declines have failed to drop below the origination points of the peaks, at least until the precipitous drop with the onset of the October 1987 crash. As Lindsay stated, the pattern was not supposed to be fail-safe. With a better than 60 percent accuracy rating, it could be regarded as a substantial improvement over the assumption that irregular markets do not exhibit any pattern whatsoever, as was previously accepted.

In the next chapter, we shift our focus from charts and patterns to a study of averages and other market and stock price indicators from both the technical and fundamental analysis disciplines.

# 3

# Market and Stock Indicators

Many investors put a lot of store in economic and stock indicators which purport to foretell the direction of the overall stock market and individual stocks. Each indicator has its advantages and shortcomings. Some possess better track records and more avid followers than others, but a knowledge of each can't but benefit any serious investor. Sift through the following array of indicators to find which will work best with your investment strategy.

## ODD LOTS

Strictly speaking, an odd lot is any number of shares bought or sold in blocks of one to 99 in contrast to a round lot of 100 shares or multiples thereof. Odd lot traders tend to be individuals since institutions possess the financial resources to purchase shares in round lots and thus avoid the odd lot differential transaction charge plus benefit from lower commissions charges.

However, since many individual investors cannot afford to purchase 100 shares of a $50 stock and still maintain a sufficient degree of diversification in their portfolio, they tend to buy in odd lots, 10 to 20 to 30 each shares of several different stocks.

In theory, the odd lot investor (construed as relatively unsophisticated) invariably makes the wrong investment decision. In order to profit from the unwise choices of odd lot investors, other investors sell when odd lotters buy and vice versa.

Odd lot believers follow changes in the ratio of odd lot buying volume to odd lot selling volume in order to discern a shift in buyer sentiment. Others track the ratio of short odd lot sales to total odd lot sales or total odd lot transactions (both sales and purchases) to round lot volume on the New York Stock Exchange.

While the methods may vary a bit, the basic theory contends that more savvy investors should start to purchase when the general public, as evidenced by odd lot trades, begins to increase its sale of stocks and vice versa. The psychology of the odd lot investor leads him or her to sell near market bottoms and purchase near market tops, good signals for the odd lot watcher.

Detractors point out that the percentage of trades by odd lot investors in relation to the market as a whole has dropped dramatically over the years and, therefore, the odd lot theory no longer applies. On the other hand, while conceding the drop in odd lot trades, supporters of the odd lot theory counter that the psychology of the individual odd lot investor remains the same regardless of the volume of odd lot activity.

## BARRON'S CONFIDENCE INDEX

The Confidence Index represents another "smart money" versus "dumb money" indicator that attracted quite a bit of attention in the investment community in years past. Published in *Barron's*, the weekly indicator reflects the difference in yields on bonds.

Originally established in 1932, the Confidence Index calculates the ratio between the average yield of the 10 highest-grade corporate bonds and the average yield on the 40 lower-quality bonds which comprise the Dow Jones Bond Average.

According to the Confidence Index theory, bond buyers represent large investors with immediate access to excellent research (smart money) and the ability to outmaneuver the market by taking or repositioning their holdings three to four months ahead of the general public investing in the stock market.

A feeling of confidence by the "smart money" people gets expressed in a move from higher quality to lower quality bond issues. In the other extreme, a mood of pessimism causes this "smart money" element to take a more conservative investment stance with a shift toward higher-grade bond investments from lower-grade bonds.

Thus movement of the Confidence Index to a more conservative stance indicates that a bear market may be in the making. Should the index exhibit a higher degree of positive influences, a rally or market upswing may be in the cards.

Typically, followers of the Confidence Index consider a reading above 88 as positive indicating better times ahead while a reading below 70 spells uncertainty and pessimism.

Detractors point out that if the so-called "smart money" could really predict future market moves, they certainly would not continue to invest in bonds but would move their portfolios en masse to the stock market where fortunes could be made on the coming bull market.

## ADVISORY SENTIMENT INDICATOR

Another confidence measurement, the Advisory Sentiment indicator measures the degree of optimism or pessimism exhibited by investment advisors.

According to Advisory Sentiment Indicator theory, the higher the ratio of bulls to bears in the investment advisory universe, the more bullish it is for the stock market until extreme optimism foretells of a market drop. Likewise, a preponderance of bears in the investment advisor community spells extreme pessimism and signals an upcoming rally.

In general, Advisory Sentiment readings above 75 percent reflect extreme optimism and a warning to be on the lookout for a sharp pullback in stock prices, while readings below 40 percent indicate the existence of extreme pessimism and the possibility of a stock market rally from an oversold position.

Refer to the Figure 3-1 Advisory Sentiment Index compiled by *Investors Intelligence*. As illustrated by the chart, the Advisory Sentiment Indicator appears to closely relate to movement in the Standard & Poor's 500 Index.

## SHORT INTEREST INDICATOR

Still another "smart money" investment theory, the Short Interest Indicator compares the ratio of short interest for a specific month to average daily market volume for the underlying security.

When certain investors are pessimistic about a stock's future price potential, they sell it short, expecting to repurchase the shares at lower prices as the market realizes its current overvaluation.

Conversely, followers of the Short Interest Indicator believe that a large short position is bullish for the stock's future price performance. On the other hand, a small short position reflects a bearish scenario.

Even though the short seller takes a pessimistic stance on the particular stock, a heavy short selling position represents significant future demand for that stock since the shorted stock will eventually have to be purchased to replace the borrowed stock. In the eyes of the short interest follower, the larger the short position, the greater the demand pressure to drive up the stock price.

In addition, a market rally or upswing in that particular stock's market price could create a "short squeeze" situation, in which short sellers will have to scramble to close out their positions, thus creating even more demand to drive the stock price even higher and force

Figure 3-1
Advisory Sentiment Index

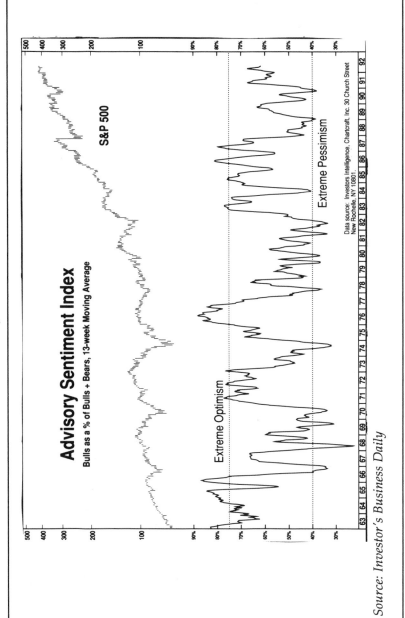

## Advisory Sentiment Index
**Bulls as a % of Bulls + Bears, 13-week Moving Average**

S&P 500

Extreme Optimism

Extreme Pessimism

Data source: Investors Intelligence, Chartcraft, Inc. 30 Church Street
New Rochelle, NY 10801.

*Source: Investor's Business Daily*

other short sellers to cover. The result is heavy demand, forcing prices up sharply and generating significant gains for those who accurately predicted and acted on the short squeeze scenario.

Short interest also serves as an indicator of the degree of market pessimism. Believers point to the surge in short interest positions near market bottoms, signalling a turnaround in the near future. Short sales traditionally rise as the Dow Jones Industrial Average declines and fall as the Dow advances.

To calculate the Short Interest Ratio for a specific stock, divide the average daily volume into the monthly short interest. For example, if XYZ Corporation's average daily volume for the month of October totaled 42,000 shares and its short interest stood at 63,000 shares, then its ratio would calculate out to 1.5. In other words, the short position represents one and one-half days of trading in the firm's stock.

The stock exchanges release short figures monthly that are readily available in *Barron's*, *Investor's Business Daily* and *The Wall Street Journal*.

Going from "smart money" to even "smarter money", proponents of the specialist short sale ratio stress that since floor exchange specialists make their living trading stocks, they make fewer mistakes or they would no longer be in the business.

A specialist short sale ratio below 40 percent signifies a bullish market, while a ratio around 65 percent or above takes on a bearish tone. To calculate the specialist short sale ratio, divide the number of shares shorted by specialists for a specific week by the number of shares shorted by the market in total. Again, the numbers are readily available in financial publications.

## INSIDER TRADING

If insiders are bullish enough to increase their stake in the fortunes of the company, what better indicator exists? Conversely, if insiders own little company stock or are reducing their holdings, why should other investors have faith in that company's future financial and stock price prospects?

Looking at the selling side of the equation, on the surface insider selling can be an indication of trouble ahead. However, caution is in order. Some insider selling stems from purely personal decisions, completely unrelated to the future direction of the company and its earnings possibilities. For example, an executive or director may need to generate cash to finance a new home purchase or to finance his or her children's college expenses or even to pay Uncle Sam's tax bill.

The decision to sell can also be the result of the desire to lock in significant stock gains from stock options exercised at prices substantially lower than current market prices.

Some followers of insider trading indicators feel that insider sellers are not normally motivated to sell since they don't have large out-of-pocket costs associated with their stock accumulations. Taking that one step further, they consider insider selling mainly in relation to the overpriced situation of the company stock and therefore a bearish signal. Obviously, several insiders shedding company stock hold more weight than a single seller. Likewise, the number of shares sold in proportion to the person's holdings also carries weight in the insider trading analysis.

On the aggregate, proponents of the insider theory track the insider sales ratio, computed as insider sales divided by insider purchases. In general, if the 10-week moving average calculates to less than 1.5, insiders are selling company shares at a slow pace, a positive sign. However, if the ratio rises above 3.0, insiders have become heavy sellers and evidently feel their firm's shares are overvalued.

Over the years, a number of studies have shown insider trading to be a fairly accurate predictor of future stock prices and a way to earn above-average investment returns. As reported in the *Journal of Economics* (1986, Vol. 16), the most comprehensive insider trading research, which covered 60,000 transactions between 1975 and 1981 (by H. Nejat Seyhun, University of Michigan), confirmed excess returns for insider purchases.

Even more interesting, those insiders with the greatest access to company information—such as the chairman of the board, officer/directors, and other board members—exhibited the greatest amount of excess returns.

For example, while chairmen of the board earned a cumulative excess average return of 3.3 percent over 100 days, a company officer only earned an excess return of 1.5 percent. That lends credence to the theory that the more knowledgeable an insider is about the overall affairs of the company, the more likely he or she is to make the right trading decisions and be a dependable predictor of future price trends.

Peter Lynch, former manager of the Magellan Fund, plays this angle a bit differently. He looks for insiders further down the corporate line for a vote of confidence in the firm. He places more faith in several vice presidents, each purchasing 1,000 shares, than in the president purchasing several thousand shares.

The Seyhun study also found that insider trading excess returns varied by company size. Firms with capitalization under $25 million earned as much as 7 percent excess returns versus only 1.2 percent excess returns for firms over $1 billion in capitalization.

Overall, insiders tend to be net sellers, selling around 2.3 shares for every 1 share they purchase. For information on insider transactions, consult either *Vicker's Weekly Insider Report, The Insiders* or Standard and Poor's *The Outlook* as well as *Barron's, Investor's Business Daily* and *The Wall Street Journal*.

The most prominent inside buyer is the company itself. While not technically an insider, its move to repurchase company shares signals the management's trust in the company to generate returns greater than that available from other potential uses of corporate cash.

The share buyback also works to reduce outstanding shares, boosting earnings per share results, a key determinant in share prices.

## ACTIVE LISTS

Since the list of actively traded stocks typically represents only about 1 percent of the overall issues traded and can account for 10 to 15 percent of the trading volume, backers of the active lists indicator stress it makes sense to be aware of and track the trends flowing from the active lists.

Noting price trends of the active popular and unpopular stocks on the list can point out shifts in investor sentiment. This can contribute to advance warning of industry groups currently moving in or out of favor, the future direction of the market as a whole and, the potential of individual securities.

The appearance or disappearance of stocks in specific industry groups documents changes in market leadership, representing shifts in market sentiment. If the trend continues for several weeks, proponents of the theory recommend actively tracking the price direction of both the industry and individual stocks with chart trendlines. In addition, recognition of chart patterns and the application of other technical analysis techniques aid the investor in uncovering buying and selling opportunities.

If the prognosis of market direction and industry group positioning proves correct, it makes sense that the most active stocks stand to make the greatest moves in the desired direction. The use of active list information, in conjunction with other technical analysis tools, can help the investor ferret out the right stocks for purchases or short selling.

The appearance on the most active list of a particular stock or several stocks in one industry signals explosive interest that the investor can utilize to generate excess investment returns.

Complementing the most active list, the most percent up in price list shows which stocks are making the biggest price surges and the percent volume change behind that price thrust. Locating a stock on both the most active list and most percent up in price indicates the stock has an extremely active following, translating into major price moves. (See Figures 3-2, 20 Most Active NYSE Stocks and 3-3 20 Most % Up in Price.)

In Figure 3-2, a preponderance of bank stocks (Citicorp, Bank America Corporation, Bank of Boston, J.P. Morgan & Company, Chemical Banking, and Chase Manhattan) make up over 25 percent of the companies on the list. All of them declined on either stable or rising trading volume.

Likewise, Figure 3-3 carries a heavy weighting of health care and energy stocks (Molecular Biosystems, Healthsouth Rehabilitation, American Oil and Gas, Anadarko Petroleum, Seagull Energy, American Health Properties) with strong price gains, most on good volume increases. This could indicate stock price recovery from an

**Figure 3-2**
**20 Most Active NYSE Stocks**

**20 Most Active NYSE Stocks**
**(Average price of 20 most active = $35)**

| EPS Rnk | Rel Str. | Stock Name | Closing Price | | Change | Group Str. | Volume (1000s) | Vol. % Change |
|---|---|---|---|---|---|---|---|---|
| 66 | 49 | Glaxo Hldgs Plc | 26⅛ | – | ⅝ | E | 2,473 | +26 |
| 98 | 53 | Telefonos De Mex L | 46⅝ | + | ⅞ | C | 1,932 | –18 |
| 83 | 92 | Citicorp | 20¾ | – | ⅜ | A | 1,612 | 0 |
| 64 | 84 | Ford Motor Co | 45¾ | + | ⅞ | A | 1,601 | +7 |
| 94 | 5 | Adv Micro Devices | 8½ | + | ¼ | D | 1,592 | +38 |
| 33 | 21 | Federated Dept Strs | 12⅞ | + | ¼ | D | 1,508 | +65 |
| 68 | 64 | General Motors Crp | 41¾ | + | ¾ | A | 1,447 | –33 |
| 28 | 57 | I B M | 97⅞ | + | ¼ | C | 1,193 | –21 |
| 73 | 66 | BankAmerica Corp | 43 | – | ¼ | A | 1,145 | +8 |
| 96 | 23 | Boeing Co | 39⅝ | + | ⅝ | C | 1,144 | +9 |
| **76** | **97** | **Bank Of Boston** | **24⅛** | – | **¾** | **A** | **1,089** | +77 |
| 64 | 59 | Morgan J P & Co | 61½ | – | ⅛ | A | 1,086 | +90 |
| 91 | 61 | Merck & Co | 50⅜ | | .... | E | 1,078 | –45 |
| **83** | **89** | **Chemical Banking** | **37¾** | – | **1⅛** | **A** | **1,056** | +11 |
| 94 | 71 | Computer Assoc Intl | 12⅛ | – | ⅜ | E | 1,049 | +92 |
| 7 | 30 | Arkla Inc | 9⅞ | + | ⅛ | B | 964 | +99 |
| 32 | 90 | Chase Manhattan | 27⅞ | – | 1⅛ | A | 957 | +51 |
| 94 | 38 | R J R Nabisco Hldgs | 9⅝ | | .... | D | 955 | –48 |
| 91 | 56 | Disney Walt Co | 34⅛ | – | ⅜ | D | 935 | –50 |
| 43 | 64 | Amer Tel & Tel | 43¾ | + | ⅛ | C | 933 | –36 |

*Source: Investor's Business Daily*

**Figure 3-3**
**Most % Up in Price**

**20 Most % Up In Price**
**(Stocks Over $12)**

| EPS Rnk | Rel Str. | Stock Name | Closing Price | Net Up | Group Str. | Volume (100s) | Vol. % Change |
|---|---|---|---|---|---|---|---|
| 94 | 12 | Callaway Golf | 23⅝ | + 2¼ | B | 204,5 | +351 |
| 12 | 15 | Molecular Biosystm | 23¾ | + 2⅛ | E | 183,5 | +365 |
| 60 | 22 | Healthsouth Rehab | 22¾ | + 2 | E | 169,7 | +11 |
| 95 | 9 | Jenny Craig Inc | 17¼ | + 1⅜ | B | 102,0 | +16 |
| **94** | **1** | **North American Mtg** | **13⅛** | **+ 1** | **A** | **256,1** | **+594** |
| 78 | 13 | Crawford & Co Cl B | 19½ | + 1⅜ | A | 52,9 | +72 |
| 75 | 28 | Smckr JMCoClB | 26¾ | + 1⅞ | C | 7,7 | −21 |
| 89 | 36 | Hilb Rogal Hamilton | 12¼ | + ¾ | C | 7,2 | −63 |
| 44 | 68 | American Oil & Gas | 12⅜ | + ¾ | A | 19,8 | −59 |
| 90 | 75 | Luxottica Group Adr | 30¼ | + 1¾ | D | 13,3 | −61 |
| 15 | 43 | H R E Properties | 13¼ | + ¾ | B | 9,3 | +31 |
| 41 | 49 | Anadarko Petrol | 25⅜ | + 1⅜ | A | 546,0 | +241 |
| 98 | 22 | Ogden Projects Inc | 19 | + 1 | E | 42,6 | +105 |
| **48** | **85** | **N W N L Companies** | **41¼** | **+ 2⅛** | **A** | **216,7** | **+561** |
| 96 | 64 | Amsco Intl Inc | 22⅞ | + 1⅛ | D | 205,2 | +97 |
| 6 | 49 | Seagull Energy | 26 | + 1¼ | A | 122,8 | +367 |
|  | 53 | Brazil Fund Inc | 18½ | + ⅞ | A | 138,0 | +36 |
| 92 | 34 | Family Dollar Stores | 15⅞ | + ¾ | E | 77,5 | −61 |
| 57 | 39 | Amer Health Pptys | 29⅝ | + 1¼ | B | 103,4 | +127 |
| 89 | 74 | Heilig−Meyers Co | 30⅜ | + 1¼ | B | 26,8 | −64 |

*Source: Investors' Business Daily*

oversold position or renewed interest in the industry and the individual stock's future prospects.

While one day's activity does not constitute a trend, pieced together with additional days' and weeks' data it can form a picture of future trends. Also, cross-checking the industry most active and percent up lists from exchange to exchange can help determine if the move is across the board or isolated to a particular market or capitalization.

Followers of action on the active list generally use the data from several weeks to construct a Most Active List Moving Average Index to focus in on the trends. It is considered bullish if the moving average continues to make new highs with gains in the market or resists making new lows in a declining market, and bearish if the moving average fails to make new highs in an advancing market or makes new lows in a receding market.

## ADVANCE/DECLINE (BREADTH) INDICATOR

Tracking the ratio of advances to declines points to market direction. As a general rule, when the net indicator rises to a positive three or above it's bullish for the market, and when the net indicator falls to a minus three or below it's bearish for the market.

Others construct the advance/decline line to track the action of the market and discern future trends. In order to plot your own advance/decline line market barometer, subtract the declines from the advances to arrive at your first chart plot. Next, add or subtract the next day's advance/decline difference from the previous day's number to arrive at the second chart plot. From then on, you add or subtract the current day's advance/decline difference from the previous cumulative total. (See Table 3-1 Determination of Chart Plots.)

To achieve the best results from use of advance/decline data, plot the advance/decline line on the same chart as the Dow Jones

### Table 3-1
### Determination of Chart Plots

| Day Number | Advances | Declines | Difference | Cum. Total/ Chart Plot |
|------------|----------|----------|------------|------------------------|
| 1 | 350 | 300 | +50 | +50 |
| 2 | 325 | 320 | +5 | +55 |
| 3 | 275 | 375 | −100 | −45 |
| 4 | 300 | 350 | −50 | −95 |
| 5 | 310 | 340 | −30 | −125 |
| 6 | 275 | 375 | −100 | −225 |
| 7 | 250 | 400 | −150 | −375 |

Industrial Average and other indexes such as the Standard & Poor's 500 and New York Stock Exchange Composite as well.

If the above averages are rising in tandem, the market uptrend should continue in force. Along the same line, if the averages are declining and the advance/decline line also shows a negative trend, the bear market is in full force. However, if the advance/decline line starts to reverse direction from the averages, be alert for a turn-around in the overall market thrust.

Often, the Dow Jones Industrial and other market averages continue their upward ascent despite the market's losing steam and eventually reversing direction. The advance/decline breadth indicator helps investors avoid being caught up in the euphoria of a rising Dow in the face of worse times ahead. In favor of this breadth indicator, most major tops have been marked by a divergence of the Dow Jones Industrial Average and the advance/decline line path. This parting of the ways can occur anywhere from a month to a year or more in advance of the market reversal.

The first reported use of the advance/decline market breadth indicator originated in the 1920s by Cleveland Trust Company economist, Colonel Leonard Ayers. Thirty years later James Hughes popularized the breadth indicator in an investment newsletter for the Wall Street firm of Auchincloss, Parker & Redpath.

Even later, Harvey A. Krow developed an advance/decline ratio by dividing the advances by the declines. Employing 10-day ratios, some advance/decline followers use a variety of ratio percentages to project additional uplegs, declines, or other market shifts.

## MOVING AVERAGE OSCILLATOR

Technically, the moving average is an analytical device for smoothing out a series of values over time. It consists of the sum of stock prices or market averages divided by the number of individual items. It derives its "moving" designation from the fact that it is constantly updated by adding a new number and dropping the oldest number in the series and recalculating the average.

To obtain the best use of moving averages, technical analysts compare them against the market in general, specific indexes, industry groupings, or other stock universes.

For example, the moving average of stock prices for Chrysler Corporation might be analyzed in comparison to the Dow Jones Industrial Average, the Standard & Poor's 500, other individual automotive industry stocks such as General Motors, the automotive industry group averages, and/or a universe of cyclical stocks.

While the moving average can be tracked in tabular form, a chart more clearly illustrates the average's trend and its relationship to other benchmarks.

Moving average technicians consider it a good sign if the moving average's trendline stays below the Dow Jones Industrial Average. When the moving average crosses and rises above the Dow, it signals a bearish condition.

Moving averages are also used to check a stock's current action against its own historical trend. In this instance, both the stock's moving average and current price get plotted on the same chart. Trading rules indicate a buying opportunity when the stock line breaks through the moving average trendline on the upside.Be prepared to sell when the stock line drops below the moving average path.

The moving average and accompanying trendline helps the investor determine the stock or average's primary direction. In theory, the length of the moving average in any one direction indicates the level and degree of strength behind the interest in the stock or amount of momentum behind the market averages. Since the moving average combines a number of different prices or averages, it smooths out the effect of a sudden move in one direction or the other, thereby reducing the risk of getting tricked by false market signals or getting whipsawed by conflicting market moves.

Two major variations of calculating the traditional moving average include the doubly smoothed moving average and the exponentially smoothed moving average. Double smoothing breaks up historical prices into subintervals, with each of these being averaged before moving into the final averaging calculation. Exponentially smoothing weights more recent prices more heavily than more dated prices.

Determining the proper length of the moving average is crucial to tracking market trends. Many technical investors use two or more moving average lines (5-day, 20-day, 100-day) in order to prevent interpreting wrong signals from temporary blips in the shorter moving average plots.

Double moving average systems signal a buy situation when the rising shorter moving average line crosses the longer moving average line. When the declining shorter moving average line breaks through the longer moving average line, it indicates a time to sell.

In addition to the moving average crossings interpretations, technical analysts also employ the three-step reversal technique and the percentage change method. In the three-step reversal technique, a downtrend is predicted with the occurrence of three declines from a previous high. Or three increases from a previous bottom identifies an uptrend. The three-move scenarios help eliminate false signals from just one or two thrusts.

The percentage change method uses specific percentage changes above or below the moving average line as a predictor of up-trends or downtrends.

An enhancement to the moving average analysis, the oscillator is a line at the base of a chart that tracks the movement of prices around a midpoint line within a historical price range. The purpose of the oscillator is to help the investor determine how fast prices are changing, in other words, the amount of momentum behind the price advance or decline.

As the price change momentum increases, the momentum line pulls away from the midpoint line, upward for advancing markets and downward for declining markets. (See Figure 3-4 Bar Chart with Oscillator.)

According to moving average theory, an oscillator warns when the market enters an overbought or oversold condition, depending on which price range boundary line the momentum line touches.

**Figure 3-4**
**Bar Chart with Oscillator**

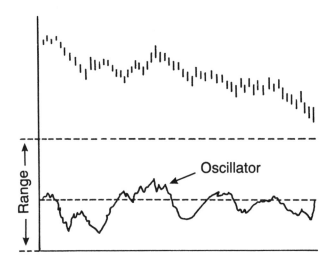

## RELATIVE STRENGTH

Another momentum indicator, relative strength, disregards price levels as such and instead concentrates on changes in price as an indicator of whether the market action signifies an acceleration or deceleration of recent movements.

Relative strength measures the price difference between specified time intervals. For example, a 15-day momentum value is derived by subtracting the price 15 trading days ago from the current price. In theory, the greater the momentum in a particular direction, the more likely the market will continue in that direction.

The relative strength index will assume new values as the rate of price movement changes. If price changes occur at a constant rate, no change will take place in the index. The momentum value line floats above or below a zero value. Buying opportunities are signaled when the momentum line rises above a buy/sell range and vice versa for selling signs.

As with moving averages, technical analysts construct charts with exponential averages and oscillators to refine the relative strength analytical tool. It can be used to compare a stock's performance with other stocks, the industry average performance and its own internal strength (whether it is gathering steam or losing momentum).

Taking a macro approach, technical analysts have used the relative strength of the Dow Jones Utility Average to predict future moves of the Dow Jones Industrial Average.

Since the level of and changes in interest rates are often a key factor in determining stock prices, the Dow Utility Average, which is comprised of 15 interest-sensitive utility stocks, provides early market direction warnings. Utilities often reflect changes in the interest rate environment quickly because they typically have large debt positions, must tap the debt market frequently, and pay high dividends. (See Figure 3-5 Utilities Average.)

For over the past 25 years, the Dow Jones Utility Average tended to move in advance of the Dow Jones Industrial Average by some two to three months. It successfully forecast the October 1987 crash peaking above 227 in early 1987 and then backtracking the rest of the year; however, it proved less prophetic prior to the October 1989 Crash.

## VOLATILITY INDICATOR

Volatile markets tend to cast off false signals, leaving investors confused, or even worse, getting them to make the wrong investment choices with disastrous results.

Normal ranges establish parameters beyond which prices or averages must move in order to distinguish the action from typical fluctuations encountered in a volatile market. The downside of using normal ranges lies in forfeiting investment gains while waiting for the price movement confirmation.

**Figure 3-5**
**Utilities Average**

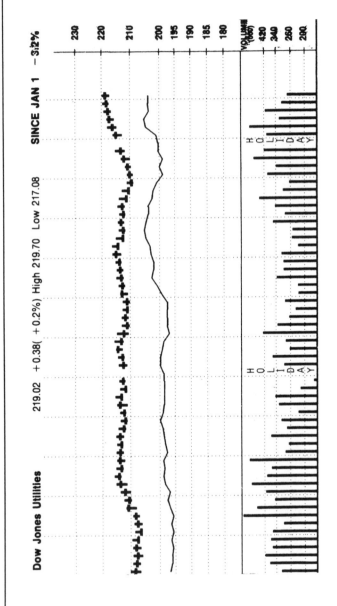

**Dow Jones Utilities**      219.02   +0.38( +0.2%) High 219.70   Low 217.08      **SINCE JAN 1   −3.2%**

*Source: Investor's Business Daily*

Volatility measurement works to eliminate that disadvantage by detecting buying and selling opportunities between the high and low levels of the price range within which a volatile stock or commodity trades.

The theory calculates the standard deviation of price movements to establish the variation of a price around an average or mean price. Volatility enthusiasts use the standard deviation to estimate the probability of future prices moving away from the average.

## VOLUME INDICATOR

An increase in volume in conjunction with stock price moves adds strength and momentum in the direction of the move. It reflects the market's confidence that the uptrend will continue in force, or its pessimism that the downtrend will.

For the overall market, declining volume as the market rises is supposed to warn of the end of a bull market. Likewise, sharp volume increases resulting in selling climaxes signal the end of a bear market.

An increase in abnormal volume can alert investors to coming price movements, up or down, before it becomes obvious to the overall market. Therefore, the market axiom "volume precedes price."

Historically, the majority of bull markets have originated with at least two days within a two-month period where upside volume is at least nine times greater than downside volume. Investors who track volume and spot the two-day Exceptional Upside Indicator can outmaneuver other investors and earn excess returns by positioning themselves for the coming bull market.

Basic volume theory includes the following maxims:

♦ Increasing volume with an advance is bullish

♦ Decreasing volume with a decline is bullish

♦ Increasing volume with a decline is bearish

♦ Decreasing volume with an advance is bearish

◆ A market top is imminent when heavy volume occurs with little or no gain in the averages

◆ Heavy volume confirms the direction of price breakouts from a support or resistance zone

◆ An increase on heavy volume after a previous substantial rally signals a "blow-off" with an impending top and reversal approaching.

◆ Heavy volume accompanied by an accelerating drop in prices confirms a "selling climax" and impending price reversal after the panic selling subsides.

◆ Low volume periods after upward price reversals reflect a consolidation phase before resumption of the upward movement.

The Daily Volume Indicator measures extremes in the supply/demand relationship. If a stock closes at the midpoint of its trading range for the day, the indicator reflects no change. Closing prices above or below the trading range midpoint show an increase or decrease in the Daily Volume Indicator, respectively.

In constructing the Daily Volume Indicator, technicians take into account the day's volume, closing price, distance between closing price and midpoint, and the trading range.

Followers cite the Daily Volume Indicator's apparent ability to mark key reversals in investor sentiment. According to this volume theory, if the price closes at the top of its trading range on heavy volume one day and at the bottom of its trading range on heavy volume the next day (or vice versa), the indicator forms a warning spike.

Other volume indicator tools include total volume line charts showing support for the direction of the market move, negative volume indicators showing price trends as volume decreases, positive volume indicators showing price trends as volume increases, and accumulation/distribution indicators illustrating the acquisition or divestiture of stock by "smart money" in advance of price moves.

In pursuit of volume predictors, technicians employ equivolume charting methods, which attempt to graphically show the interrelationship between price movement and volume. Equivolume charts place heavy emphasis on price spread and volume and give little weight to closing prices.

While the typical bar chart places volume information at the bottom of the chart with a separate scale, equivolume charting lifts the volume data off the chart base and incorporates it into the price plottings. (See Figure 3-6 Bar Chart with Volume and Figure 3-7 Equivolume Chart.)

In contrast to the bar chart, which represents each trading day as a line, the equivolume chart uses a rectangle with the width of the triangle showing the trade volume across the horizontal axis instead of time. Each trading day is indicated within the box. The top and bottom of the rectangle show the day's high and low trading points. Unlike bar charts, equivolume charts do not indicate closing prices.

The width and height of the rectangle reflect the impact of volume on each day's price action. The wider the box, the heavier the volume. A narrow box (taller than wide) reflects ease of movement in the stock's price. Likewise, a wide box indicates resistance to price moves.

## THE ARMS INDEX (SHORT-TERM TRADING INDEX or TRIN)

Developed by Richard W. Arms Jr., the Arms Index contends that knowledge of volume is just as important as price movement in understanding the markets. As in equivolume charting, volume takes on the significance of a full partner with price.

Originally, the Arms Index applied only to the New York Stock Exchange when revealed in the late 1960s. Since then, applications have been expanded to the American Stock Exchange and over-the-counter market.

To construct the Arms Index, first divide the number of advancing issues by the number of declining issues (A). Next, divide ad-

**Figure 3-6**
**Bar Chart with Volume**

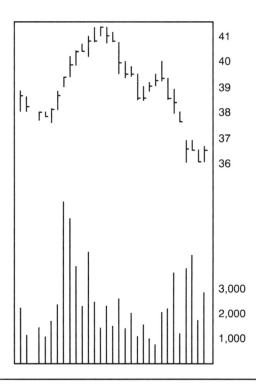

vancing volume by declining volume (B). Finally, divide (A) by (B) to arrive at the day's Arms Index or TRIN.

For example, the Arms Index value for a day with 520 up stocks, 600 down stocks, and 5,200,000 advancing volume and 6,400,000 declining volume would calculate out to 1.07.

$$(520/600) \ / \ (5,200,000/6,400,000) \ =$$
$$(.867) \quad / \ (.811) \qquad\qquad = 1.07$$

If the index tops one, the average volume of stocks that fell was greater than the average volume of stocks that rose; the opposite is

**Figure 3-7**
**Equivolume Chart**

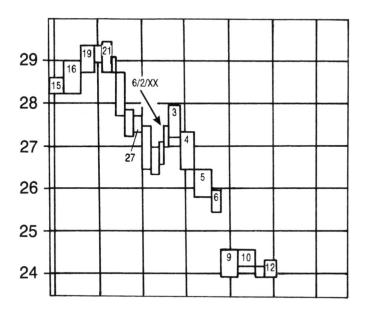

true if the index comes in under one. An index of one represents a standstill market in terms of direction since the volume of up stocks equals the volume of down stocks.

A reading in excess of one forecasts a bearish thrust since the largest proportion of volume is associated with stocks that are declining. On the other hand, a reading less than one, reflects a bullish trend with advancing stocks garnering the most volume.

The Arms Index can be used to help uncover short-term trading opportunities as well as to forecast long-term movement trends. Long-term traders should not be overly concerned with intra-day moves except in the building or liquidating of positions. Look to the 55-day moving average of the index for the best indication of oversold or overbought market conditions.

## THE COLUMBIA LONG-LEADING COMPOSITE INDICATOR

As discussed in Chapter 1, the Commerce Department's Index of Leading Indicators ranks as the most widely followed predictor of the overall economy. However, in the late 1980s, another index came on the investment scene.

Developed by economists at Columbia University's Center for International Business Cycle Research, the new "Columbia Index" purports to predict long-term economic movements.

Its founders claim their index possesses the ability to provide timelier warnings of major turning points in the business cycle compared to other economic indicators. Using reconstructed data, the Columbia researchers determined that their long-leading composite signaled recessions on average four months in advance of the Commerce Department's Index of Leading Indicators. (See Figure 3-8 Columbia Index Months Advance Warning.)

Of the Columbia Index's four components, two also compose part of the Commerce Department's index; money supply and the number of new housing units evidenced by building permits. The other Columbia Index components are a monthly average of Dow Jones 20-bond price index and a ratio of price to labor costs in manufacturing.

## THE W.O.W. INDEX

Developed by Weiss Research, Inc. in West Palm Beach, Florida, the W.O.W. (Who Owns What) Index expands on market sentiment theory by tracking the owners of specific investment types. According to this indicator, if an investment is held by "strong hands," the likelihood of a sudden flurry of selling remains small. Any news, either

**Figure 3-8**
**Columbia Index Months Advance Warning**

| RECESSION | COMMERCE INDEX | COLUMBIA INDEX |
|---|---|---|
| 1948-49 | 10 | 7 |
| 1953-54 | 4 | 8 |
| 1957-58 | 23 | 27 |
| 1960-61 | 11 | 11 |
| 1969-70 | 8 | 10 |
| 1973-75 | 8 | 10 |
| 1980 | 10 | 27 |
| 1981-82 | 3 | 10 |
| AVERAGE | 10 | 14 |

*Sources: Commerce Department; Columbia Center for International Business Cycle Research.*

good or bad, will tend to trigger a rise. On the other hand, if held by "weak hands," the direction of the move will most likely be down.

This strategy combines elements of both the "strong hands" (insiders) and "weak hands" (odd-lot buyers), looking for significant imbalances between the two groups and/or visible departures from the normal trading patterns.

## MUTUAL FUND CASH POSITIONS

Changes in the level of mutual fund cash positions are also regarded by some as predictors of investment sentiment by major players exerting a significant influence on the direction of the market. Measured as the percentage to total mutual fund assets held in cash and cash equivalents, the greater the percentage of cash the more bullish for the market and vice versa. High cash positions are believed to represent future demand with the potential to drive up stock prices.

As a general rule, a cash position ratio of 10 percent or more is considered bullish, while a drop below the 5 1/2 percent cash level signals a bearish trend. As backup for the theory, historical evidence shows mutual funds have tended to be fully invested near market tops and carry relatively high cash positions near market bottoms.

Even though the mutual fund investment managers are supposed to represent "smart money," this tendency has earned them the reputation as the "Institutional Odd-Lotters."

## THE HADADY BULLISH CONSENSUS

Originally developed by Earl Hadady of Hadady Publications, publishers of *Contrary Opinion* in Pasadena, California; the Bullish Consensus indicator attempts to uncover overbought or oversold conditions in the commodities market. Based on a weekly survey of advisors and extensive research in commodity markets, Hadady graphs the Bullish Consensus along with the commodities price movement.

In addition, Hadady uses a Consensus Meter to determine the significance of consensus readings. (See Figure 3-9 Hadady Bullish Consensus Meter.)

For example, if 90 percent of the survey holds a bullish opinion, the market represents a significantly overbought position with a sharp downward price reversal predicted. Likewise, a 10 percent bullish consensus reading foretells a severely oversold situation and a sharp upward price reversal.

## THE MARKET LOGIC DAILY COMPOSITE INDICATOR

Taking a much shorter predictor stance, the Market Logic Daily Composite Indicator works to foretell the direction of the next day's market. Originally developed in 1979 for *Market Logic*, an investment advisory newsletter published by The Institute for Econometric Re-

**Figure 3-9**
**Hadady Bullish Consensus Meter**

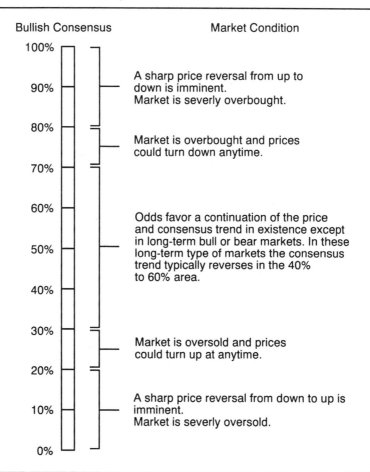

Bullish Consensus

Market Condition

100%

90% — A sharp price reversal from up to down is imminent.
Market is severely overbought.

80%

Market is overbought and prices could turn down anytime.

70%

60%

Odds favor a continuation of the price and consensus trend in existence except in long-term bull or bear markets. In these long-term type of markets the consensus trend typically reverses in the 40% to 60% area.

50%

40%

30% Market is oversold and prices could turn up at anytime.

20%

A sharp price reversal from down to up is imminent.
10% Market is severely oversold.

0%

search in Fort Lauderdale, Florida, and later slightly modified by Gerald Appel and W. Frederick Hitschler in *Stock Market Trading Systems* (Dow Jones-Irwin,1980), the Daily Composite indicator involves taking five stock market readings on a daily basis.

According to the Market Logic theory, the number of plus readings corresponds to percentage probabilities that the market will rise on the next trading day, as illustrated by Table 3-2.

Reading components and their measurement include:

1) Advance/decline numbers. If more issues advance on the New York Stock Exchange than decline, mark a plus reading.

2) Trend. If the daily reading of advances less declines tops the previous day's net advance/decline calculation, mark a plus reading.

3) TRIN. TRIN calculations of less than one are bullish; mark a plus reading. (See Arms Index [TRIN] earlier in this chapter for a discussion of the TRIN calculation).

4) TICK. The net amount of trades occurring on upticks. Mark a plus if there is a positive tick reading for the day.

5) Seasonality. Mark a plus reading if the next trading day occurs on a Friday, the last trading day of any month, the first four trading days of any month, or the two days prior to a market holiday.

### Table 3–2

| Number of Plus Readings | Probability of Next Day Market Rise |
|:---:|:---:|
| 0 | 23% |
| 1 | 29 |
| 2 | 50 |
| 3 | 66 |
| 4 | 78 |
| 5 | 90 |

Use the sum of the plus readings for each day as a predictor of the probability of an up market on the next trading day as shown in the table above.

## NEW HIGHS/NEW LOWS

Similar in function to the advance/decline breadth indicator, the New Highs/New Lows technical predictor measures whether or not the number of new highs and new lows are expanding or declining. New highs represent the number of issues that have reached new highs during the latest 52-week period and vice versa for new lows.

Simply put, an expanding list of new highs bodes well for the market, while additions of new lows sends a bearish signal. Of course, technical analysts also consider other factors in their prognosis.

For example, the current market phase and whether or not any divergence exists between the new high/new low indicator and market averages can influence the analysis. If the Dow Jones Industrial Average moves on to post new market highs while the number of new highs starts to drop or plot a series of declining peaks, a potential reversal lies ahead. During a bear market, a noticeable decline in the number of new lows as the Dow continues to plummet alerts the investor to a possible upturn in the near future.

Other market reversal warning signs include an increasing number of new lows while the Dow moves upward and an increasing number of new highs as the bear market proceeds.

Tracking the new high/new low information can take several forms. Some investors prefer keeping moving averages of both the new highs and new lows, while others gravitate toward tracking the net difference between the new highs and new lows.

Norman G. Fosback, author of *Stock Market Logic* (The Institute for Econometric Research in Fort Lauderdale, Florida), developed the High/Low Logic Index in 1979. As originally presented, Fosback's index can be used for data from either the New York Stock Exchange or the American Exchange. The index is computed as the lesser of either new highs as a percentage of the issues traded or new lows as a percentage of the issues traded.

Typically, either a significant number of new highs or new lows would occur, but not both. Using the lesser value for the index helps insure that high readings would be difficult to achieve under normal market circumstances. Therefore, a high index reading would indicate a period of extreme divergence in the market with many stocks establishing new highs and new lows.

Since investment markets thrive on uniformity, the High Low Logic Index considered a high reading (above 5 percent) to represent extreme market divergence and therefore a bearish sign. Readings below 1 percent were considered to show market uniformity and a bullish indicator. Historically, a rare double-digit reading preceded precipitous declines in market prices and the start of major bull market moves.

## SPECULATIVE INDEX

This predictor is based on the premise that investors move from the more solid investments to more speculative securities as the market heats up and approaches a top. The assumption that more lower quality and therefore speculative issues reside on the American Stock Exchange than on the New York Stock Exchange lies at the heart of this prediction theory.

Traditionally, stock market action moves in tandem with investor sentiment or moods. Investors react to the economy and markets running through cycles of depression, extreme caution, building confidence, bullishness, speculation, overspeculation, bearishness, back down to depression—starting the cycle all over again.

As speculation heats up, investors shift from sound investments and stocks with proven track records to the stocks touted as the next "big winner." This move to more speculative investments coincides with a shift to more activity on the American Stock Exchange in relation to the New York Stock Exchange. For this reason, investors closely follow the "Speculation Index" developed in the 1960s by the *Indicator Digest*.

A high speculation reading (higher volume on the American Exchange relative to New York Exchange) indicates a move toward over speculation and a market reversal ahead. A low reading indicates a concentration on investment quality and wariness of speculative issues, a good sign for a market upturn and sustained bull market. The lower the reading, the closer the market is to a bottom. Conversely, the higher the index, the closer the market is to a top.

Technicians use a moving average (15-weeks or more) to help smooth out weekly fluctuations that tend to distort the trend. On a historical basis, the Speculation Index has ranged from a low of 10 percent to a high around 60 percent. Readings in the 10–15 percent range have preceded strong bull markets, while readings around 50 percent typically occur before major bear markets.

In recent years, some technicians believe the Speculation Index has lost some of its glitter in the wake of a decline in the volume of American Exchange trading activity with the rising popularity of options trading.

## MARGIN REQUIREMENTS/MARGIN DEBT

Trends in margin requirements and margin debt levels portray the amount of capital/credit available for investment and the degree of investor sentiment behind market moves.

The Federal Reserve Board uses margin requirements to temper the increase of speculative activity by raising or lowering the amount of money investors can borrow to purchases securities. Substantial margin debt in the 1920s contributed heavily to overspecualation and the resulting stock market crash. In recent decades, margin levels have ranged from a high of 80 percent to a low of 50 percent, where it currently resides.

With 50 percent margin requirements, investors can purchase twice as much stock for the same capital investment by borrowing from their brokers and depositing the required collateral in cash or securities. The use of margin delivers substantial leverage capability to the investor, allowing him or her to earn a much higher rate of return.

Increases in the margin requirement forces investors to put up more of their own cash, thus placing a damper on speculative activity and the rise in stock prices. Conversely, an easing of margin requirements allows investors to purchase more securities with less cash up front, creating more investor interest and demand and higher stock prices.

While margin requirement changes have been few and far between lately—the last one took place in 1974—it's wise to keep a proper perspective of the results of past margin requirement changes.

The Federal Reserve Board's actions to decrease speculation by raising margin requirements have historically produced an initial dampening effect on stock market prices. This has been followed by a period of recovery and rising market prices up to a year or more after the Fed's action, before the more stringent margin requirements take root and initiate a general market decline.

The Fed's moves to turn around significant market downturns with margin requirement decreases has for the most part signalled upcoming market bottoms. While the initial market reaction to the easing of margin requirements usually takes on a negative tone, with the stock market dropping over the first fifteen days, by the end of a year and a half, the market has moved up substantially.

Margin debt refers to the amount of money owed by customers to New York Stock Exchange member firms in order to finance additional purchases of stock. With margin investors considered "smart money," the higher the level of customer margin debt, the more bullish the market scenario. On the other hand, lower levels and decreasing margin debt signify that the "smart money" players are liquidating their positions, a bearish indicator.

Margin debt grows significantly during bull markets and shrinks during bear markets. Tracking the level of margin debt can help signal the direction of the market.

A recent example occurred in 1974. Margin debt hit a low of $3.84 billion, while the Dow Jones Industrial Average plunged over 45 percent, from a high of 1051.70 in 1973 to a low of 577.60 in 1974. By 1987, margin debt peaked at $44.17 billion for a better than 1,000 percent increase. Likewise, the Dow surged to a 1987 high of 2,722.42 top before falling victim to the October Crash.

Construction of a 12-month debt margin moving average and a trendline of current debt margin can help determine market direction. When the current trendline breaks above the moving average line, a buy signal is indicated. On the downside, when the current debt margin line plunges below the moving average line, it issues a bearish sell signal.

Taking a look at the ratio of margin buys to margin sells, high buy/sell ratios have a history of foretelling market peaks and following bear action. The readings hit high levels in advance of the 1980, 1983, 1987 and 1989 market drops.

## DIVIDENDS, YIELD, P/Es AND THE STANDARD & POOR'S 500

A bevy of predictor systems flow from the historical relationships between market direction and the levels of dividends, yields, price/earnings ratios and the Standard & Poor's 500 Index.

As stock prices rise rapidly in a fast-paced bull market, stock dividend levels and their yields tend to lag behind. Historically, nearly every time that the average yield on common stocks for the S & P 500 fell below 3 percent, a bear market ensued, with the market declining. For example, in 1987 after the average dividend yield dropped below 3 percent to 2.68 percent, October shocked the market with a precipitous crash.

The dividend yield for the S & P 500 is considered average, around 3.6 percent. Market bottoms can be anticipated when the dividend yield average rises to the 4 percent or greater. Refer to Table 3-3 for average dividend yields at market bottoms over the past two decades.

**Table 3-3**
**Market Bottom Dividend Yields**

| Market Bottom | Average Dividend Yield for S & P 500 Stocks |
|---|---|
| 12-4-87 | 4.0% |
| 7-24-84 | 5.2 |
| 8-12-82 | 6.9 |
| 3-06-78 | 6.0 |
| 10-3-74 | 5.9 |

Another method of gauging market tops with dividend levels calculates the stock price-to-dividend ratio. This represents the number of dollars investors are willing to pay for one dollar worth of dividend. As stock prices increase and the dividend yield drops a larger percentage of the investor's overall investment, return must be made up by capital gains. Some technicians warn of an approaching market top when the price-to-dividend ratio nears 30-to-1.

Comparing high-yield to low-yield stocks, in general higher yielding stocks will not decline as much in a bear market as stocks with lower dividend yields since the dividend yield works to support the stock price.

The earnings yield (aggregate per share earnings divided by the S & P 500) of the S & P 500 can be used in comparison with the yield on 3-month Treasury Bills to detect warning market turns. Followers of this predictor start looking for a bear market when the S & P 500 earnings yield falls below that offered by three-month T-Bills. On the upside, a rise of two percentage points above the T-Bill yield is considered bullish.

The price/earnings ratio is calculated by dividing the earnings per share into the stock market per share price. Many investors follow the overall market price/earnings ratio, as evidenced by the S & P 500 in efforts to discern overbought or oversold conditions.

According to this prediction system, the lower the market price/earnings ratio, the more likely the market is approaching a bottom. Since 1953, the average market bottom price/earnings ratio calculates out to just under 11, with lows of 7.0 in 1974, 8.0 in 1978, 7.6 in 1982, 8.9 in 1984 and 11.5 in 1987.

Price/earnings ratios in excess of 20 are considered unsustainable and indicative of impending market declines.

Finally, the S & P 500 itself sends warnings signals when the composite index breaks through the trendline for its 12-month moving average on the downside. Each time this has happened in the past century, either a bear market or a period of considerable consolidation ensued.

## MONETARY INDICATORS

An increase in the money supply (M2) bodes well for the stock market. Theoretically, additional money in the hands of investors should translate into higher demand, pushing up stock prices. In addition, the M2 impact on the overall economy indirectly affects stock market results.

Since World War II, whenever real M2 growth has turned negative, the economy shifted into a recession, after lags of different lengths.

Recent detractors point out that the low short-term interest rates experienced in the early 1990s make the M2 gauge less reliable than in the past. The reason for this is that investors have shifted their liquid assets out of money market funds and bank accounts which are included in M2 into bond and stock mutual funds which are not included in M2, resulting in a distortion of the traditionally reliable index.

An easy to follow Treasury Bill rule contends that when the yield on these securities rises above 6 percent, the market will decline, and when the yield falls below 6 percent, the market will advance. The theory is based on the premise that tight money and increasing interest rates will eventually halt a bull market and reverse market direction. As interest rates increase, funds are with-drawn from the market, creating a demand/supply imbalance and driving down stock market prices.

Use of the Treasury Bill as an indicator derives from its apparent ability to lead other short-term instruments in interest rate changes by a month or two.

Increases or decreases in the discount rate (the rate the Federal Reserve charges member banks) often impact the stock market. Discount rate hikes frequently precede bull market peaks, while cuts in the discount rate spur economic activity, push other interest rates downward, and precede market bottoms.

With a good grasp of the economy, business cycles, technical analysis and market predictors in hand, it's time to move to some investment theories.

# 4

# Investment Theories

There's a myriad of broad based investment theories within which numerous investment strategies can be implemented. This chapter will look at the rationale behind these theories and how they work. Chapter 5, Investment Strategies, will delve into the particulars of specific investment strategies. As you will see, some theories support the logic behind certain strategies, while other theories negate the possibility that a particular strategy will prove successful.

## EFFICIENT MARKET THEORY

Contrary to technical analysis and value investing, the Efficient Market Theory contends that the investment markets are so efficient that all public information regarding a company or its stock gets immediately reflected in its stock price. Based on this premise, there exists no opportunity to discern future market trends or uncover hidden value situations. In other words, a truly efficient market makes it impossible to make trading profits through the use of publicly available investment information, no matter how recent. Since not all investors buy into the pure efficient market scenario, three different forms have developed over the years:the weak, semistrong, and strong hypothesis.

In the weak form, stock prices are assumed to reflect a randomness, with the next trading price likely to be up or down. Historical prices and patterns exert no influence whatsoever on future prices or price direction. While the weak form does admit the possibility of earning above-normal investment returns with a combination of trading strategies, it cannot be accomplished using past prices alone.

Also known as the Random Walk Theory, the weak form gained prominence in the 1960s in the wake of numerous research studies. Much of the work culminated in findings similar to the Brownian Motion Theory found in the physical sciences. Market price variances over time were considered independent of each other, just as minute particles suspended in solution moved independently of each other.

In 1973, Princeton professor Burton G. Malkiel gave Random Walk almost a cult status with his book *A Random Walk Down Wall Street* (W.W. Norton & Company, Inc. latest edition, 1990). Malkiel provides three characteristics of the efficient market. First of all, an efficient market responds very rapidly to new information. Second, since stock prices are assumed to reflect all available information, it is impossible for investors to use that information for beating the market. Third, investors can't beat the market except by chance.

In essence, Malkiel claims that the market does not reward information, since it has already been discounted in the stock price, but it does reward risk-taking. Using this risk-taking strategy approach, Malkiel sets out several investment strategies, from out-of-favor stocks to small and neglected stocks.

The semistrong hypothesis says that stock prices accurately reflect all publicly available information regarding a company. All information regarding the firm's balance sheet, earnings, dividends, etc., have already been taken into account in the company's current market price. New information on companies, industries, the economy, and so on arrive in a random fashion; therefore, changes in stock market prices also take on a random pattern. It then follows that since the resulting changes in price occur randomly, investors cannot use the information to earn above average returns.

In the efficient market-strong form, no information, either public or private, can help investors consistently earn higher rates of return without assuming greater degrees of risk.

Others have modified the Efficient Market Theory to explain that random pricing does not have to imply the absence of any rational price formation. Under this version, stock market prices are determined by the firm's earning power, market share, products, dividends, and other fundamental factors, but the randomness in pricing stems from investors' inability to accurately forecast changes in those factors and their impact on stock prices rather than solely on the market's efficiency in absorbing information.

This runs counter to the "dartboard mentality" (anyone picking stocks by throwing darts at the financial pages can outperform investors using systems or investment strategies) inherent in the efficient market hypothesis. However, over the years, many dart board portfolios have outperformed the professional money managers.

Whether you subscribe to the Efficient Market Theory in any of its forms or not will have an enormous impact on how you tackle the market.

## CYBERNETIC ANALYSIS

Jerry Felson offers an alternative to the efficient market theory in his book, *Cybernetic Approach to Stock Market Analysis* (Exposition Press, 1975) in order to bypass its perceived limitations and deficiencies.

According to Felson, the extreme complexity of the stock market and the environment in which it operates as well as inadequate investment tools hamper the investor from earning above-average investment returns.

Using cybernetics concepts (the science and control of communication, and mathematical analysis of the flow of information) and artificial intelligence (advanced cybernetics) techniques, Felson proposes developing judgmental decision-making processes by weighing evidence and formalizing investment analysis.

In plain language, the cybernetics approach automates the investment decision-making process through the use of pattern recognition, learning system theory, and other methods, removing the imperfect human factor and theoretically improving investment returns.

Felson stresses that no investment analysis can be very successful unless it conforms to the law of requisite variety. In other words, the investment decision system must be as complex and as variable as the system (stock market) which it is trying to interpret. According to Felson, this is where other investment systems fail.

While cybernetics cannot yet replace the human factor, it claims to offer better insight into investment analysis than otherwise available and to allow for the development of new investment techniques for superior performance.

## CASTLE-IN-THE-AIR THEORY

The Castle-in-the-Air Theory ignores investment intrinsic values and looks to the interpretation and prediction of investor sentiments and actions in order to make their investment positions before the crowd. Lord Maynard Keynes, a respected economist and successful investor, expounded on the theory in 1936. He reported on how investors gravitated away from the hard work of determining intrinsic value to discern how the investing public will act in the future as they build 'castles in the sky' based on their hopes and dreams.

Instead of using investment valuation techniques, followers of this theory tried to divine the psychology of the market and where it was headed. It made no difference if a stock currently priced at $25 per share possessed intrinsic value of $30 per share if investors had a negative opinion of the company and their declining demand for the stock would drive its price down to the $20 per share level. Correctly anticipating that market sentiment and shorting the stock would be the proper investment move under the Castle-in-the-Air theory.

Examples of excess mass psychology upsetting all semblance of economic order and rational investment behavior range from the unprecedented surge in gold prices during 1980, when gold rose above $840 per ounce, to the Dutch tulip bulb panic in 1637. Understanding how the crowd thinks and reacts in both normal circumstances and panic situations can deliver a big edge to investors willing to study individual and crowd psychology in relation to the stock market. Market psychology and the herd instinct often play a leading, if not major role in the determination of stock prices and market direction.

Popular investment approaches that use investor psychology as a base include odd-lot theory, contrarian investing, consensus indicators, etc.

Some strategists have even gone so far as to classify investors into specific investment personalities. One such model considers investors falling into one of five classifications ranging from straight arrow to careful to confident to anxious to impetuous, based on personality characteristics such as exhibiting confidence, anxiety, or caution.

Knowing your own personality make-up and how it relates to the investment markets can also help improve your chances of success. Dr. Sully Blotnick, a research psychologist and author of business-related books, developed a profile of the successful investor. According to his theory, the most successful investors tend to concentrate their investments in a narrow range of investments or stocks. Contrary to popular opinion, concentration, not diversification, provides the success edge. Of course, you must balance the degree of risk you are willing to assume with the opportunity for greater returns.

Another trait of the successful investor is the ability to stick with their investment choices and let their profits run. On the other hand, unsuccessful investors tend to follow fads and sell out too soon. Finally, successful investors tend to invest in what they know, industries and companies with which they are already familiar.

## FIRM FOUNDATION THEORY

While the Castle-in-the-Air Theory focuses on investment psychology, the Firm Foundation Theory seeks to uncover the investment's underlying, or intrinsic, value.

Back in 1934, John Burr Williams discussed the major determinants of intrinsic value as the basis for the firm foundation theory in his book, *The Theory of Investment* (North-Holland Publishing Company). He took into consideration such items as future earnings, future dividends, market interest rate levels and projections, marketability, growth possibilities, merger and internal expansion prospects, inflation, and the political and economic scenario.

According to the theory, buying opportunities exist when the stock price falls below its intrinsic value, and selling opportunities present themselves when the firm's stock price rises above its intrinsic value. A monitoring of the intrinsic value with current stock price levels can help the investor achieve superior investment returns.

In searching for intrinsic value, the Firm Foundation Theory evaluates the expected earnings growth rate, the expected dividend growth rate, the expected dividend payout, market interest rates and the degree of risk.

While the Firm Foundation Theory makes perfectly good sense, its shortcomings stem from the inability of investors to make accurate projections about future company, monetary and economic events. The degree of error in these assumptions obviously impacts the return on investments based on these predictions.

## MARKOWITZ PORTFOLIO SELECTION THEORY

In March 1952, Harry Markowitz published his "Portfolio Selection" treatise in the *Journal of Finance*. Markowitz contended that portfolio selection must take into account both expected return and the degree of portfolio risk. This risk included not only the risk inherent in the individual investments comprising the portfolio but also the risk derived from the interrelationships of those individual securities.

He theorized that rational investors strive for efficient portfolios that maximize expected return for a certain degree of risk or minimize risk for a specific expected return. In addition, Markowitz believed efficient portfolios were attainable through the careful analysis and evaluation of a security's expected return, the variation in that return, and the relationships between each security's return and the returns of other securities.

Graphically, Figure 4-1 Efficient Portfolios illustrates the range of efficient portfolios for different levels of expected return and degrees of risk. Points A, B, and C along the curve represent the most efficient portfolios because they deliver the highest rate of return for a specific degree of risk or the least amount of risk for a desired rate of return.

**Figure 4-1**
**Efficient Portfolios**

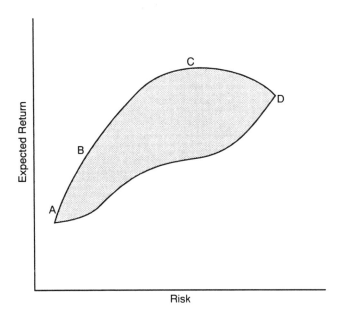

The shaded area corresponds to the universe of available securities or investment options. Point D fails the efficiency test because other points along the curve offer the same return at lower risk levels.

As with other theories, Markowitz's Portfolio Selection Theory must exist in an imperfect world where expected returns do not materialize, degrees of risk get miscalculated, and investors do not always choose the risk-adverse option.

## BERNSTEIN'S PSYCHOLOGY OF SUCCESSFUL INVESTING

In contrast to Markowitz's rational investor who seeks the most risk-adverse investment position, clinical psychologist and commodities trader Jacob Bernstein views humans as speculative beasts by nature. In his book, *Investor's Quotient: The Psychology of Successful Investing in Commodities & Stocks* (John Wiley & Sons, 1980), Bernstein links psychology and successful trading.

According to Bernstein, the ultimate success of each individual lies less in his or her investment strategy and more in the make-up of the person.

Along those lines, Bernstein constructed a questionnaire designed to help individual investors determine if they have what it takes to be a successful trader. While he states that the test questions derive from his own experience and are not validated or standardized, evaluation of the answers in comparison with profiles of successful traders can provide some insight into problem areas and the need to reassess certain investment actions or reactions.

According to findings from Bernstein's survey, most successful traders do not subscribe to more than a few advisory services (the emotionally weak investor tends to draw advice from too many sources); those who expect too much from a broker usually get disappointed (brokers should be used for efficient execution and quick response time and not investment advice); it is the mark of a successful trader to plan investing strategy well in advance; successful traders use stops effectively; the most successful traders buy and hold for the long term; the most successful traders recognize the importance of isolation to block out interfering information and the opinions of others; and those who set aside specific time for studying the markets and investment opportunities fare better.

The development of a positive mental attitude (PMA) ranks high on Bernstein's list of effective techniques for successful trading. In fact, he traces periods of high PMA to situations where the person takes on a positive self-concept, everything goes well and profits increase. Conversely, periods of low PMA correspond with poor future outlooks, an increase in mistakes and rising losses.

Practicing PMA as a way of life increases the individual's ability to avoid, ignore or eliminate negative influences and experiences. Bernstein recommends a three-step process to achieve a change from a negative to a positive mental attitude: recognition, initiation of change, and internalization and maintenance.

## TOP DOWN INVESTING

There are two basic overall strategies for approaching the investment decision-making process: the top down approach and the bottom up approach. Each one takes a considerably different path to making the eventual investment decision.

Top down investing first concentrates on analyzing the big picture before moving downward toward choosing the individual security in which to invest. Taking the macro approach begins with an investigation and analysis of the economic environment. (Depending on the expertise of the investor, available investment resources, and the overall investment goal, the economic analysis could be limited to the domestic economy or expanded to include a global focus.)

The investor also works to gain a perspective of projected interest rates, anticipated economic growth rates, changing tax and monetary policies, the competitive environment, political factors, and the direction of the stock market.

Next, the investor turns to an analysis of which industries and/or market segments stand to benefit or suffer most from the most likely economic and political scenario. For example, in the wake of warming relations between the East and West, future revenue and earning prospects for many defense firms quickly eroded. A correct prognosis of this emerging situation could have positioned an investor to short stocks of specific companies heavily dependent on defense business and most likely to be negatively impacted by slashed defense budgets.

Moving from the industry analysis, the investor reviews the prospects of individual firms in order to make the best investment choice.

## BOTTOM UP INVESTING

The opposite extreme, bottom up investing, takes a micro approach, starting with the investment fundamentals of the individual stock before moving upward to include an analysis of the industry environment, overall economic factors, and other factors that could impact the prospects of the company.

The bottom up approach focuses on individual stock selection, looking for stocks that are undervalued the most and are positioned to prosper and perform best in the future. For example, a bottom up investing strategy could help discover a fast rising company with increasing revenues and earnings such as Hauser Chemical, a company with surging operating results and rising stock prices. Spurred by lucrative contracts to supply Taxol, a cancer treatment material developed from the rare Yew tree. Hauser's stock price rose from a 52-week low of $6 1/2 per share to a high of $27 1/2 per share in 1992.

Unfortunately, for investors who ignored competitive and technological factors the company's stock plunged to less than $14 per share in the wake of the introduction of an alternative new source of Taxol produced without destroying the rare Yew tree.

While industry, sector, and economic factors take on less importance than the company's fundamentals, such as earnings growth, in the bottom up investing strategy, the savvy bottom up investor goes beyond the company's fundamentals in order to make an informed investment decision and avoid costly mistakes that jeopardize investment returns.

## DIVERSIFICATION

One of the long standing and most prevalent risk-reducing investment strategies involves creating a diversified portfolio. In essence, diversification can take four basic forms: stock portfolio, geographical, strategy and total asset. Without diversification, investors lay themselves open to unnecessary risk that could be possibly be prevented or at least reduced by spreading their investments among different stocks, investment types, market sectors, industries, geographical locations and engaging in strategy diversification.

### *Rule of Eight*

The "Rule of Eight" amply explains the stock portfolio diversification strategy. Under this premise, a minimum of eight stocks are required to properly achieve enough diversification to prevent the occurrence of an unpredictable event to any single stock proving to be disaster for your portfolio.

There are plenty or risks that can negatively impact the market performance of any stock. Prolonged labor unrest, natural disasters, technological advances, fraud, lawsuits, unfavorable legislation, etc. can cause company's financial performance to tumble, forcing down its stock price with a vengeance. While any of these risks and more can happen to any of your stocks, the likelihood of them happening to more than one at the same time is greatly reduced through diversification.

Therefore, limiting the amount of money percentage wise into any one stock ranks as a top investment strategy and wealth preserver. The lack of sufficient financial capital to purchase at least eight stocks often arises as a reason for not employing diversification. Under the "Rule of Eight" premise, if you cannot afford eight different stocks then stay out of the market for individual stocks. However, you can participate in the stock market by gaining your diversification through a stake in a mutual fund.

### Geographical Diversification

In recent years, geographical diversification has become more available to individual investors. While previously virtually limited to geographical diversification within the domestic United States and Canada, today's U.S. investor can now choose from a bevy of foreign securities due to the proliferation of American Depository Receipts (ADRs). In addition, the introduction of a flurry of global and international mutual funds in recent years enhances the level of geographical diversification available to investors.

ADRs are negotiable receipts held in the vault of a United States bank and represent ownership in the shares of a foreign corporation. They entitle investors to trade them just like stock on United States stock exchanges and over-the-counter market. ADR owners are entitled to all dividend and capital gains just like stockholders. The use of ADRs eliminate the necessity for American investors to trade on complicated foreign stock exchanges.

Currently, more than 900 foreign securities trade as ADRs in the United States from companies all over the globe, offering substantial opportunities for greater geographic diversification. Major ADR originations include the United Kingdom, Australia, Germany, France and, more recently, Mexico. Other ADRs come from a variety of places including Singapore, Italy, The Netherlands and Spain. Investor interest in ADRs continues to grow with more than $85 billion in trading volume in 1991.

John P. Dessauer, a geographical diversification advocate and author of *Passport to Profits* (Dearborn Financial Publishing, 1991) believes in putting at least 25 percent of your stock investments in companies outside of the United States. You can achieve this through the use of ADRs or investing in mutual funds which invest exclusively in overseas securities.

Among successful mutual funds which have moved into the global and international investing arenas are Templeton with its Emerging Markets Fund, Alliance Global Small Cap, Merrill International Holdings and Paine Webber Atlas. For those looking to create their own geographical diversified mixture of mutuals, funds families have created more specialized geographic investment options such as Paine Webber Investment-Europe Region, Merrill Pacific, Mexico Equity & Income Fund and Growth Fund of Spain.

### Strategy Diversification

Strategy diversification involves the application of various investment strategies over time. While the stock market has far outperformed other investment alternatives over the long run, there have been and will continue to be time frames during which bonds, gold, collectibles, etc. have turned the tables and earned higher returns than generated by stocks.

Certain investment strategies work well in some stock market and economic environments and not in others. Even the most historically successful investment strategies fail at times. As strategies and theories become more well known and popular they tend to lose some of their ability to deliver above normal returns.

Diversifying among different investment strategies and rotating your strategies as market and economic conditions change can help reduce your investment risk and increase your investment returns.

### Total Asset Diversification

Total asset diversification seeks to view the investment portfolio as a whole with percentage holdings of stocks, real estate, precious metals, fixed income instruments (both short and long term), collectibles, and savings accounts.

With asset diversification, the investor can accomplish a balanced portfolio to take into account changing economic and market conditions as well as his or her risk comfort level and personal financial objectives.

Of course all risk cannot be removed from the investment decision. Some types of risk will be shared by all stocks no matter how many the investor holds.

In *The Complete Investment Book* (Scott, Foresman, 1985) Rich Bookstaber illustrates the importance of diversifying by investing in stocks with no correlation between them. Using Bookstaber's example, assume recession, normal, and boom probabilities of 30 percent, 40 percent, and 30 percent, respectively. In addition, assume Firms X, Y, and Z possess the rates of return shown in Table 4-1 Economic Probabilities, Risk, and Expected Return. Using the above information, the expected return for each firm is given at the right of the chart.

Owning firm X stock carries a higher degree of risk since the returns can swing some 16 percent and can drop to a low of 2 percent. However, the expected return of 10 percent outpaces the 8 percent offered by either firm Y or firm Z. While firms Y and Z have the same level of risk and expected return, they differ. Firm Y exhibits a cyclical pattern rising more during boom periods, while firm Z acts in a counter-cyclical manner, performing better during economic downturns.

**Table 4-1**
**Economic Probabilities, Risk, and Expected Returns**

| | Return | | | |
|---|---|---|---|---|
| | Recession | Normal | Boom | Expected Return |
| Probability | .3 | .4 | .3 | |
| Firm | | | | |
| X | 2% | 10% | 18% | 10% |
| Y | 4% | 8% | 12% | 8% |
| Z | 12% | 8% | 4% | 8% |

Instead of holding just one firm's stock, risk can be reduced by diversifying and holding two different stocks in the portfolio. Table 4-2 Diversification Effect illustrates how owing equal amounts of either firms' X and Y or firms' X and Z stock may or may not reduce risk.

In the case of firms X and Y, the companies are highly correlated, and thus the combination still carries a high degree of risk, with returns ranging from a low of 3 percent to a high of 15 percent. On the other hand, the firms' X and Z combination reduces the risk substantially with a return spread of only 4 percent, with a low of 7 percent and a high of 11 percent. Equally important, the expected return only decreased 1 percent.

As Bookstaber illustrates, blindly following the diversification strategy for its own sake may not achieve the desired risk-reducing results.

### Asset Allocation

Inherent in the diversification strategy discussed earlier, asset allocation seeks to minimize investment risk with a spreading of portfolio assets among different investment type alternatives.

Given an investor's risk tolerance and investment goals, an asset allocation strategy can be constructed to deliver the desired return within the risk parameters. The asset allocation method uses normal ranges for each class of investment and adjusts the portfolio as re-

### Table 4-2
### Diversification Effect

|  | Return | | | |
|---|---|---|---|---|
|  | Recession | Normal | Boom | Expected Return |
| Portfolio |  |  |  |  |
| X and Y | 3% | 9% | 15% | 9% |
| X and Z | 7% | 9% | 11% | 9% |

quired to maintain that balance and take advantage of unique investment opportunities. The allocation ranges vary depending on the individual investor's risk tolerance, investment goals, age, and financial circumstances.

Recommended asset allocation ranges for investment assets include 5–35 percent in cash, 10–40 percent in fixed income securities, 20–60 percent in equities and 5–20 percent in inflation hedges.

Also called the multi-asset, total return concept, asset allocation seeks to offer the flexibility of earning the best possible total return within a variety of different economic and market environments. For example, investment portfolios during inflationary periods would be more heavily weighted with real estate and precious metals holdings near the top end of their range.

During a sluggish economy, with low inflation and low interest rates as took place in the early 1990s, some investment strategists recommended a shift to intermediate bonds to collect favorable yields without the capital risk associated with longer fixed income investments. Other strategists preferred defensive stocks such as utilities, telephone companies and insurance companies. Still others believed the economy was in the early stages of a recovery and opted for a heavier mix of cyclical stocks.

For the investor not confident enough or too busy to make his or her own asset allocation decisions, mutual fund families have developed asset allocation funds such as the Blanchard Strategic Growth, Dean Witter Managed Assets, Dreyfus Strategic, Paine Webber Asset Allocation, Prudential FlexiFund-Strategy, and Shearson Equity-Strategic Investment mutual funds.

For a graphic presentation of the asset allocation strategy refer to Figure 4-2 Asset Allocation Pyramid. Investors need to take into consideration their age, need for liquidity, financial situation, tax situation, risk tolerance, and investment goals in the construction of their own asset allocation pyramid.

For example, a young couple with small children would need a heavy weighting of growth investments to provide for future education expenses, accumulate capital for a larger home, and build net worth for their eventual retirement years. They can afford to take on more risk at this stage in their lives because they have ample time to recoup any losses.

On the other hand, safety of principal and current cash flow represent prime investment goals of retirees. They can no longer afford to face market risks in pursuit of higher than normal investment returns. In this case, a portfolio stressing safety and income could be built from a mixture heavily weighted in fixed income securities with

**Figure 4-2**
**Asset Allocation Pyramid**

Speculative
Inflation Hedges

Precious
Metals
Commodities

Growth
Equities

Growth Stocks
Funds

Growth and Income
Fixed Income

Dividend-Paying Stocks
Corporate Bonds
Municipal Bonds
Annuities

Safety and Income
Cash/(Equivalent)

Savings/Cash
Money Markets
CDs
Government Treasuries

smaller proportions of cash and cash equivalents and equities. This will be discussed further in Life Cycle Investing, later in this chapter.

The basic variable ratio plan for asset allocation consists of developing upper and lower limits for each investment type. According to theory, the ideal variable ratio plan would provide for minimum stock holdings at market peaks and maximum stock holdings at market bottoms.

Adding to and reducing positions in the asset categories occurs when the percentage of holdings in a particular asset classification moves outside of a channel at certain intervals from the median. For example, a strategy may start to reduce the stock portion of the asset allocation portfolio by 5 percent when it rises 10 percent above its median level and increase its stock assets by 5 percent when it falls 10 percent below its median level.

The variable ratio plan offers better protection against being too heavily weighted in one asset type as can occur under a constant ratio or constant dollar approach. For example, the constant approaches result in the same percentage of stocks being held whether the market is approaching a top or approaching a bottom, increasing the risks of incurring substantial losses and missing profit opportunities. Considering that the purpose of asset allocation is to increase total return and reduce risk, the variable ratio plan offers more flexibility, safety and a bigger opportunity for better than normal investment returns.

To be sure, asset allocation investors don't take Mark Twain's Pudd'nhead Wilson's words to heart, "Put all your eggs in one basket and—WATCH THAT BASKET."

## LIFE CYCLE INVESTING

As mentioned in the discussion on asset allocation, investment goals and risk posture as well as financial position change over time. These changes must be taken into consideration in building an investment portfolio. Life cycle investing theory looks at these life stages and proposes model portfolio formats designed to achieve those goals within set risk parameters.

According to life cycle investing theory, individuals travel through different life stages with different investment goals and risk tolerances associated with them. For the average investor, without taking into account the life cycle approach, the risk/return relationship would be depicted as shown in Figure 4-3 Risk Return Relationship. Each individual would have to determine for him or herself how much risk they want to assume to achieve greater returns, as evidenced by a move to the right on the risk/return line.

Typically, younger investors would take a higher risk posture to garner higher returns and build up their wealth (Point A). If losses occur, they have the time to recoup. On the other hand, older investors would stay on the lower end of the risk/return line, preferring to protect existing wealth (Point B). Their investment posture would obviously be tempered from losses incurred in earlier years.

**Figure 4-3**
**Risk/Return Relationship**

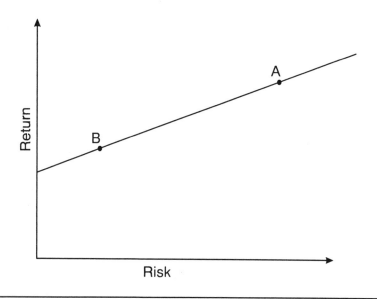

Franco Modigliani first put forward the "Life Cycle Hypothesis of Income, Consumption and Saving." His treatise contended that people move through a progression of dissaving (spending more than they earn in their younger years) to a period of net saving (as wealth increases) to another period of dissaving as they retire and live off previously accumulated financial assets.

Inherent in the life cycle theory is that certain types of investments and risk postures are more favorable for certain stages of investors' lives. The theory also recognizes the importance of early planning and anticipation of future financial commitments and cash outflows (such as college expenses). Finally, it stresses the importance of remaining flexible enough to make the appropriate changes in investments as the individual progresses from one life stage to another.

Four phases comprise the life cycle. Each phase and its characteristics are noted in Table 4-3 Life Cycle Phases and Characteristics. Follow the movement in the life cycles phases in Figure 4-4 Risk/Return Relationships at Life Cycle Phases.

According to Donald R. Nichols in his book, *Life Cycle Investing* (Dow Jones Irwin, 1985), investors must take into account five key elements in constructing a life cycle portfolio: stability of principal, current income, capital growth, aggressive income, and growth and lump sum investments.

Investors achieve principal stability by searching out investments that provide optimum protection against market loss and value fluctuations. While the investment will earn some return, the paramount consideration is to guard against loss of the principal amount.

Current income generating investments such as dividend from common and preferred stocks, bonds, certificates of deposit, and savings accounts take on more importance as investors progress through the life cycle phases.

Capital growth investments seek long-term capital appreciation to build the desired level of wealth with which to live through the retirement years, an important investment strategy in the early to mid-years of the life cycle.

## Table 4-3
## Life Cycle Phases and Characteristics

| Phase | Characteristics |
| --- | --- |
| Accumulation | Early career. Small net worth, large liabilities such as house mortgage and credit purchases, illiquid assets. Priorities include accumulating savings for new home, college expenses, etc. Higher risk posture with long-term investment horizon. (Point A) |
| Consolidation | Mid-to-late career. Best income earning years coupled with declining expenses as children leave home and house expenses taper off. Peak wealth accumulation years. Institution of more risk control to protect built up capital. (Point B) |
| Spending | Retirement years. Financially independent status. Accumulated assets cover living expenses. Low risk posture to conserve and protect assets for income generation. (Point C) |
| Gifting | Realization that accumulated assets exceed anticipated living expenses. Redirection of assets to provide for heirs or other causes. Still low-risk posture to ensure passing along assets with the exception that some people at this phase take on pet projects without regard to the amount of risk involved. |

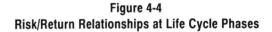

**Figure 4-4**
**Risk/Return Relationships at Life Cycle Phases**

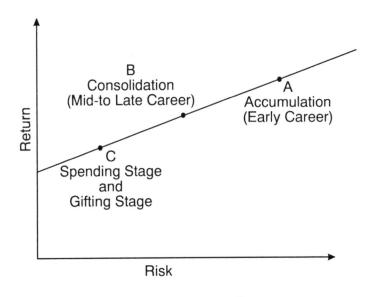

Ideal growth oriented investments include common stocks, mutual funds and bonds as well as hard assets such as real estate and precious metals. Company-sponsored pensions, profit-sharing, and savings plans also build wealth rapidly, sometimes with the company making a substantial proportion of the contributions. Individual contributions can also be made pre-tax, adding to the growth capabilities of the investment.

Aggressive income and growth investments combine higher potential returns with a higher degree of risk and are appropriate for those in the accumulation phase of the life cycle. Again, stocks, bonds and mutual funds join forces with more speculative investment alternatives such as precious metals, currencies, commodity futures, and options.

Lump sum investments provide continual growth and wealth accumulation within a specific time frame. Zero coupon investments and certificates of deposits represent popular lump sum investments. These can be utilized during any phase of the life cycle.

In addition to considering the particular stage of an individual in the life cycle process, others also look at another facet of life cycle strategy. Life cycle investing can also apply to investigating and understanding where a company fits in its own life cycle before investing in a stock.

Like people, companies also progress through different phases which have different implications for the company's future prospects. A firm can change from an aggressive growth stock to a growth stock to a mature industry stock within a period of years, depending on the industry, technological factors and other factors.

## BUY THE RUMOR/SELL THE FACT

According to this theory, by the time you know the fact, it is too late to capitalize on the information. In order to profit from the new information, the investor must anticipate market reaction based on the context of the available rumor.

Obviously, the rumor would have to set a bullish tone or else it would be foolish to purchase on the rumor. Once the investment position has been established based on the rumor, it's time to sell when the rumor gets confirmed as fact. This allows the savvy and adept investor to sell at a profit as latecomers bid up the security's market price.

To distinguish rumors from facts, the investor must consider the source of the information. Typically, but not always, facts come from reputable sources such as government or corporate reports. Usually, rumor sources are hard to identify, coming across as unknown sources.

Anticipating rumors can also lead to higher returns. Proponents of this strategy recommend keeping an eye out for trading action without accompanying facts that might signal an impending announcement of significant importance to the company's future prospects and its stock price level.

Other strategists guard against acting before the facts become known in order to prevent getting sideswiped by faulty rumors or a misreading of trading action.

## CONSTANT STOCK-BOND RATIO THEORY

The Constant Stock-Bond Ratio Theory represents one proposed method of achieving steady income while preserving capital. Its beauty lies in not having to forecast future price ranges or waiting for historical price patterns to repeat themselves.

By removing these judgmental aspects of investing, the plan works to eliminate investment decisions which might jeopardize the safety of principal. It is not a plan designed to generate capital growth or provide protection in the event of a declining market.

While a variety of Constant Stock-Bond Ratio plans exist, the basic premise rests on the predetermination of set proportions of the portfolio to be held in stocks and bonds and to maintain that proportional relationship over time with additional purchases and sales as price movements alter the proportions. The original ratio can be determined to suit the investor's particular investment goals and risk posture.

A cousin to the Constant Stock-Bond Ratio Theory, the Constant Dollar Theory takes the entire profits on stocks and reinvests them in bonds to maintain the constant dollar amount. On the other hand, the profits from stock sales are reinvested in both bonds and stocks based on the original stock-bond ratio.

For example: a $40,000 investment split equally between stocks and bonds would be adjusted as in Table 4-4.

In order to maintain the 50/50 ratio, enough stocks would have to be sold and enough bonds purchased to return the portfolio to equilibrium at $22,000 of value in both stocks and bonds.

Variations of the Constant Stock-Bond Ratio plans include valuing the bond portfolio by either par value or market value. The decision would center on the investment grade of the bonds since lower

**Table 4-4**

|  | Stock Value | % of Fund | Bond Value | % of Fund | Total Fund |
|---|---|---|---|---|---|
| Orig | $20,000 | 50% | $20,000 | 50% | $40,000 |
| 20% Rise | 24,000 | 54.5% | 20,000 | 46.5% | 44,000 |
| 50% Ratio | 22,000 | 50% | 22,000 | 50% | 44,000 |

grade and junk bonds tend to trade more in line with stocks, while higher grade bonds tend to maintain more stable prices.

The theory behind the Constant Dollar Plan stems from the desire to maintain a constant dollar level of exposure to the stock market. As stock prices rise, the investors sell off stock holdings to return to the specified dollar stock investment level. The proceeds are reinvested in bonds. Likewise, as stock prices decline, bonds are sold to purchase stocks and bring up the value of stock held to the desired dollar amount.

The Constant Dollar Plan works to ensure stocks are sold as prices rise, thus locking in gains, and stocks are purchased as prices drop, thus helping to achieve a lower average cost and an accumulation of more shares in depressed markets for big gains as the market turns around.

Modifications to either plan set certain price move limits which must be reached before any buying or selling takes place. That prevents getting whipsawed by a volatile market and also limits the number of transactions, saving on commission charges.

## SELLING THEORIES

Much has been written about how to investigate which investments to purchase and how to time your purchases to maximize investment returns. However, there has been significantly less emphasis placed on the selling side of the business.

Donald L. Cassidy, author of *It's Not What Stocks You Buy, It's When You Sell That Counts* (Probus, 1991) sets out to correct that deficiency. According to Cassidy, achieving a finely honed selling discipline is key to investment success. After all, you really haven't made any money until the moment you sell and get cash in hand. On the other hand, holding onto a dog can deliver disastrous results to your investment returns.

Cassidy recommends recognizing mistakes instead of ignoring or minimizing them. Cut your losses by selling and chalk it up to a learning experience. Keep a record of your mistakes to determine what went wrong and how you can avoid similar mistakes in the future.

In making investment decisions, Cassidy stresses that the investor's cost price is irrelevant once the purchase has been made. He considers it psychological baggage which clouds the thinking of the investor with a detrimental effect on the execution of a successful sale. According to Cassidy, a good price or time at which to sell is defined by what happens to the stock after the sale occurs and has nothing whatsoever to do with the prior event of the investor's purchase of a stock at a certain price.

To illustrate, if a stock is sold at $50 per share and then drops to $40 per share, it was a wise selling decision. It made no difference whether the investor paid $30, $40, $50 or $60 per share for the stock.

Other tips from Cassidy to help investors improve their selling discipline include separating the stock from the company (personal feelings for the company affect investment judgment); separating selling stock to raise money to make other purchases (this leads to badly timed sales); selling on news delays (most news delays often fall into the bad news category) and analyzing whether or not the stock you currently own should be purchased now at its present price (if not, then you better sell).

Gerald M. Loeb, a well-known investor, advises not to wait too long to sell. It is better to err in selling too soon than not selling at all. He urges selling on great strength and not waiting for trouble to spur you to liquidate. Use of technical indicators such as relative strength can provide advance warning signs.

Other investment strategists offer the following rules in timing your sale:

◆ Sell between one-fourth and one-half of your holding after it has tripled, followed by additional fractional shares with further substantial rises in price

◆ Reevaluate any stock for selling if it has declined 50 percent from its purchase price

◆ Sell when a merger or buyout is announced to take advantage of the suddenly higher prices. Some deals fall through and you don't want to run the risk of the stock plummeting once more to gain a few more points

◆ Forget the, "I need to get even before I sell" syndrome. It often means even more losses

Learning an effective selling discipline also means taking into account short selling opportunities to take advantage of anticipated declining prices and negative investor sentiment.

An old adage, "Sell short as often as you go long," may not be precisely correct since the market has traditionally moved to higher ground after bearish and bullish cycles. Some have adapted the saying to read, "You should be willing to sell short as well as long, but not as frequently."

## THE 10 PERCENT RULE

Intended to help the investor catch broad market swings, the 10 percent rule offers simplicity and a way to avoid making wrong value judgements which negatively impact investment returns.

Implementation of the 10 percent rule involves little more than having the investor calculate the value of his or her portfolio at specific intervals, usually a week. Then at the end of the month, the weekly figures are averaged. As long as the monthly averages maintain a rise or hold relatively steady, the investor keeps fully invested.

A drop in the monthly average of 10 percent below a previous high signals a sell situation, advising the investor to shed all holdings immediately. Of course, no new purchases are made until the 30-day average for the former holdings rises 10 percent above a monthly low. Once that happens, the investor takes a fully invested position again.

The drawback of the 10 percent rule lies in the construction of the portfolio to begin with. A mixture of blue chip stocks will perform differently than a mixture of lower quality, speculative issues. In fact, they may move in counter directions, causing the investor to miss a major market move.

## THE WINDBAG THEORY

In 1992, Jason Zweig and John Chamberlain compiled the Windbag Theory for publication in *Forbes*. While a bit tongue in cheek, it did provide a lot of food for thought and some rather convincing examples.

The basic Windbag Theory premise states that as companies start to get into trouble, telltale signs will begin to appear in their annual reports. Certainly, company financial statements often signal trouble in the making, but this theory goes beyond the annual report's numbers to review the chairman's letter to shareholders.

According to Zweig and Chamberlain, the more flowery the language, the greater the risk that the company may be headed for serious trouble. In other words, the chairman's verbosity increases in direct proportion to the severity of the company's problems.

The two even concocted the "Forbes Fog Factor" which is calculated from bombastic measures, such as the length of the chairman's letter, the average number of words per sentence, the average number of letters per word and the average of passive constructions. A sharp rise in the "Forbes Fog Factor" signals a sell situation, while a decline in the measure spells better times ahead.

# 5

# Investment Strategies

Now that we have a firm grasp of the economic playing field, technical analysis, market and stock indicators, and the breadth of investment theories, it's time to delve into some specific investment strategies based on some or all of the above.

In the pages ahead, we will take a look at a variety of value strategies, from ferreting out low price/earnings stocks to using earnings models. In addition, we'll cover other investment strategies, such as growth stock investing, dollar cost averaging, contrarian investing, Tuccille's Dynamic Investing, and superperformance investing, etc.

However, before we jump into the world of investment strategies, it's important to grasp a clear understanding of investment risk. How many types of investment risk can put a portfolio at risk? Which investments work well to minimize certain types of risk? These questions and more need to be assessed in order for the investor to build the proper portfolio able to deliver the return desired within certain risk parameters.

## INVESTMENT RISK

Investment risk can take several forms: business risk, market risk, interest rate risk, reinvestment risk, and inflation risk. Additional risk subsets such as call risk (having a bond redeemed early at unfavorable prices), political risk (unfavorable legislation), and timing risk (misinterpreting market signals) are inherent in the above major risk classifications. These and other subset risks will not be covered in this discussion except by broad reference. Needless to say, they need to be acknowledged and evaluated in the context of your investment decision-making process.

### *Business Risk*

Business risk refers to the impact that fluctuations in the economic environment and changes in other aspects of the business environment can have on the ability of the company to deliver expected earnings results and dividend payouts. A variety of factors comprise business risk, such as fiscal and monetary policy, regulatory policy, technological change, management changes, competition, product liability, etc.

A savvy investor assesses the level of business risk facing the company in which he or she wishes to purchase stock. In that assessment, the investor looks at how well the company is positioned to take advantage of certain conditions or how well the firm is shielded from certain risks.

For example, a highly leveraged company has the ability to deliver greater ROI (return on investment); however, it runs the risk of default in a contracting economic environment.

The investor needs to evaluate the ratio of financial leverage and the firm's ability to handle the extra financial burden of high leverage in changing economic environments.

### *Market Risk*

Market risk stems from the basic economic fact that market prices of investments will fluctuate for a variety of reasons including a change in the economic fortunes of the company, external events such as moves in interest rates and the outbreak of war, internal changes such as labor unrest and management changes, and a shift in investor sentiment toward the particular company or the market as a whole.

For real estate investments, market risk fluctuates with changes in tax policy, national and regional economies, interest rates, the number of existing and proposed competing properties, etc. In the precious metal arena, market risk can increase or decrease with changes in the economic environment, inflation, the level of foreign dumping of precious metal holdings, etc.

Each investment type has some risks that are unique in how they affect that investment's performance in the market. While inflation and rising interest rates make long-term bonds a less desirable holding, they work to make precious metals relatively more attractive.

### Interest Rate Risk

Interest rate risk refers to the changing cost of borrowing money. When interest rates rise, the value of existing fixed income investments declines. Conversely, when interest rates decline, the value of existing fixed income investments rises. Therefore, an investor has to assess the probability of different interest rate-change scenarios. Obviously, it would be foolish to invest in long-term fixed income securities with a stated interest rate of 5 percent if interest rates had a 70 percent chance of rising over the next several years to 7 percent or higher.

The degree of interest risk you assume in fixed income investing is closely tied to the time period of that investment. That's why longer-term investments typically pay higher yields, to compensate the investor for the additional risk he or she takes on. (See Figure 5-1 Interest Rate/Risk Relationship.) Normally, the longer the investment horizon, the higher the interest rate associated with it. (See Figure 5-2 Yield Curve.)

This is true because the longer you hold a fixed income investment, the greater the possibility of interest rate fluctuations, resulting in changes of the fixed income security's value and price in the sec-

**Figure 5-1**
**Interest Rate/Risk Relationship**

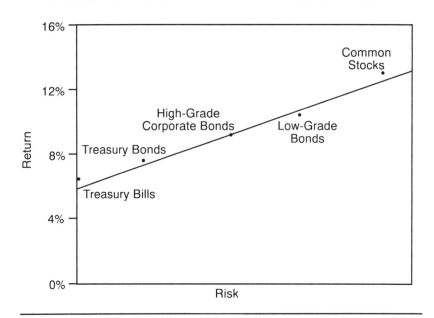

ondary market where it trades. Therefore, the closer your security gets to maturity, the less it will be affected by changing market interest rates.

However, abnormal conditions in the economic environment can result in short-term interest rates rising above that offered by long-term fixed income investments. The result is a negative yield curve. (See Figure 5-3 Negative Yield Curve.)

Traditionally, other market interest rates have been benchmarked off United States Treasury rates and are often quoted as spreads off appropriate Treasury yields. Since Treasury issues are considered top investment quality with the least risk of default, other fixed-income investments must pay a premium in the form of higher

**Figure 5-2**
**Yield Curve**

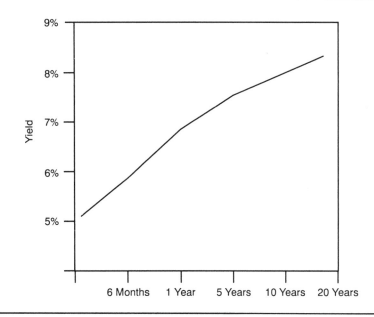

interest rates in order to attract investors away from the more secure Treasuries.

The degree of credit risk, and therefore the level of interest rates paid on specific fixed-income investments, is based on an analysis of the issuer's ability to repay the debt on time. These are evidenced in the credit ratings provided by such credit rating firms as Fitch Investors Service, Moody's Investor Service, and Standard & Poor's Corporation. Generally, the lower the credit rating, the higher the required interest rate to compensate investors for the additional risk.

Some strategists recommend using the yield curve to measure interest rate risk. The U.S. Treasury yield curve represents how interest rates rise with the lengthening of maturities. According to this

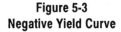

**Figure 5-3**
**Negative Yield Curve**

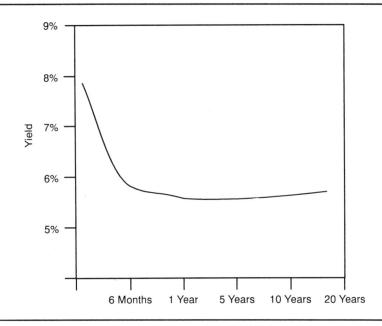

strategy, the yield spread between the shortest and longest maturities can signal the degree of investor demand for both short- and long-term investments. The wider the spread, the more investors antici-pate a reduction in market interest rates and vice versa.

The steepness of the yield curve also provides some clues. The steeper the yield curve, the easier it is for investors to increase yields substantially by moving from short- to intermediate-term invest-ments. (See Figure 5-4 U.S. Treasury Yield Curve.) With a steep yield curve as indicated in Figure 5-4, an investor can move up 2 3/4 percentage points, a nearly 70 percent jump from 4 percent to 6 3/4 percent, by extending maturities from two years to five years. The risk lies in the proper assessment that market interest rates will rise during the investment period, more than offsetting the additional gain in yield.

**Figure 5-4**
**U.S. Treasury Yield Curve**

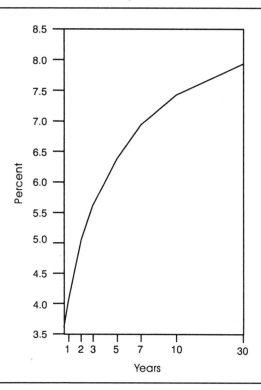

In addition to their impact on fixed-income investments, interest rate changes also impact stocks since they alter the cost, and often, the ability to finance a business's ongoing operations, expansions and acquisitions.

### Reinvestment Risk

Reinvestment risk stems from the possible inability to reinvest cash flows from investments (dividends, interest, proceeds from investment sales) at the same rate of return or yield, or higher than that offered by the original investment.

For example, as 8 percent bonds mature, current market interest rates for the same quality investment may be only paying 6 percent. The investor must then choose between accepting lower investment returns or adopting a higher degree of risk to maintain a specific yield.

This exact scenario happened in the early 1990s as short-term interest rates on certificates of deposit fell dramatically. Investors were faced with drops in yield from over 8 percent to under 4 percent within a two-year time frame. Unfortunately, too often the temptation to earn a certain return caused investors to move "from cash to trash," putting their principal in jeopardy.

One way to lessen the reinvestment risk lies in laddering your fixed-income investments with a number of different maturity dates. In that way, only a certain percentage of your fixed-income investments will mature within a given period of time.

For example, if you had $20,000 to invest in fixed-income securities, instead of using the whole $20,000 stake to purchase a bond maturing in 10 years and yielding 9 percent, you could purchase $5,000 worth each of four different bonds with differing maturities. While you may have to give up some yield on shorter maturities, you protect yourself from having all $20,000 of your bonds maturing at a time when market interest rates have fallen to 3 percent, an inopportune time to reinvest that sum of money.

### Inflation Risk

Finally, inflation risk represents the potential loss in purchasing power. This encompasses your money being worth less due to the rise in the costs of goods and services outpacing your rate of return. If inflation rears its ugly head and drives up the cost of living by 8 percent while certificates of deposit only provide a 4 percent yield, the investor turns up a net loser, defeated by the inflation risk.

Anticipating changes in the inflation environment and investing in inflation hedges such as real estate and precious metals can help negate the inflation risk and even produce substantial capital gains.

Similar to inflation risks are currency risks which can cause the value of your investment and its return to decrease with fluctuations in the relative value of currencies.

## THE RENSHAW RISK-DETERMINED FORECASTING TECHNIQUE

Edward Renshaw, a finance professor at the State University of New York, developed a stock market forecasting technique in the late 1980s taking into account risk.

According to the Renshaw strategy, 3-month Treasury Bill rates and the Standard & Poor's Utility Index helps determine a "risk premium" for the year prior to the one being forecasted. The risk premium is calculated as follows: the S & P Utility dividend yield for the prior year plus the annual dividend growth rate minus the average last-month-of-the-year yield on new 3-month Treasury Bills.

Renshaw's forecasting strategy states that if the calculated risk premium for a given year exceeds 3 percent, then the S & P 500 should deliver gains for the following year. On the other hand, a calculated risk premium of 3 percent or less means a loss for the S & P 500.

Testing of his theory found that for the years 1964 through 1984, the S & P 500 yielded a 14.6 percent average annual return in years following a year with a risk premium in excess of 3 percent. For years following a year with a 3 percent or less risk premium, the average annual returns were a negative 10 percent. During the test period, the Renshaw strategy failed to predict losses for the Standard & Poor's 500 index only twice.

## GRAHAM & DODD VALUE APPROACH

Among the original value seekers, Benjamin Graham and David Dodd developed the classic strategy of value analysis investing in their monumental book, *Security Analysis*, first published in 1934.

Graham later expanded on his value investing techniques with his book, *The Intelligent Investor*, published in 1949, listing stock selection criteria. Still later, Graham and James B. Rea revised and expanded on the original list.

Graham et al contended that certain stock selection criteria used in uncovering hidden value could help the investor earn above-average returns.

Among value stock selection criteria popularized by Graham and his colleagues over the years are the following:

◆ Current ratio (current assets divided by current liabilities) greater than two

◆ Dividend continuity over 20 years

◆ Current stock price less than 1 1/2 times book value

◆ Current stock price less than 15 times the average earnings of the prior three years

◆ Earnings-to-price yield at least twice the AAA bond yield

◆ Dividend yield at least 2/3 of the AAA bond yield

◆ Total debt less than tangible book value

◆ Total debt less than or equal to twice the net current asset value

◆ Stock price less than 2/3 of tangible book value per share

◆ Stock price less than 2/3 of net current asset value

◆ Earnings growth for the prior 10 years at least at 7 percent compounded annual rate

Since the Graham days, other investment strategists have added to and subtracted from his original value analysis strategies in order to fine tune the process. Others have zeroed in on specific portions of the value analysis concept, concentrating on price/earnings ratios, dividend models, cash flow analysis, asset evaluation, and other aspects in efforts to perfect methods for detecting undervalued situations.

In any case, the basic premise remains. Certain stock and market information can be used to detect undervalued situations which the alert investor can use to his or her advantage in earning above-average returns.

Charles S. Brandes, in his book *Value Investing Today* (Dow Jones-Irwin, 1989) stresses four benefits of employing value investing. First of all, value investing provides lower risk than growth or other investing strategies. Second, a value-based portfolio offers lower portfolio volatility. Third, a reduction in trading costs should accrue to the investor. Fourth and most importantly, historical returns show that value investing pays off in dollars and cents, outperforming the Standard & Poor's 500 benchmark.

## CONTRARIAN INVESTING, LOW PRICE/EARNINGS STYLE

David Dreman, one of the strongest and most successful proponents of contrarian investing, uses a heavy dose of low P/E research to guide his firm's, Dreman Value Management in Jersey City, New Jersey, investment decision making.

Decades of research by Dreman and others have found that low P/E investing outperforms the S & P 500 Index in good times and bad. For example, a Dreman study of returns for the period from January 1, 1966 through December 31, 1990 found an annual return of 13.9 percent for low P/E stocks versus 9.6 percent for the third P/E quartile, 8.9 percent for the high P/E stocks and only 10.8 percent for the market average. (See Figure 5-5 Dreman 25-Year P/E Study Bar Chart.)

Another contrary investing fan, Richard Band, author of *Contrary Investing for the '90s* (St. Martin's Press, 1989) stresses that people make markets, both through rational and irrational behavior. The contrarian seeks to discover the irrational behavior affecting stock prices and creating unique investment opportunities.

## Figure 5-5
## Dreman 25-Year P/E Study Bar Chart

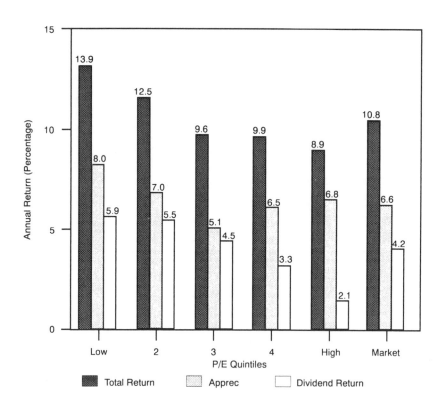

*Source:* Dreman Value Management

Band advises against getting caught up in the crowd, making investment decisions based on emotion instead of factual information. Instead, take advantage of these moments of mass delusion to take a contrary investment position.

Band offers some basic contrarian trading rules to help investors position themselves to capitalize on market overreactions created by the herd instinct.

◆ If the bullish consensus goes above 80 percent or below 20 percent, immediately position yourself against the prevailing trend.

◆ Trade with the prevailing trend until the consensus reaches the 80/20 extremes.

◆ During a strong primary bull or bear market, a short-term correction usually won't carry the consensus down to 20 percent or up to 80 percent.

Refer to Chapter 3 for a discussion of consensus and a look at Figure 3-9 Hadady Bullish Consensus Meter.

## THE PHOENIX APPROACH

Another contrarian strategy is proposed by William J. Grace, Jr., in his book, *The Phoenix Approach: The Contrarian's Guide to Profiting from Out-of-Favor, Distressed and Bankrupt Companies* (Bantam Books, 1989).

According to Grace, the contrarian believes that professional investors make predictable investment blunders and that the astute investor can take advantage of such institutional behavior.

The basic premise of the Phoenix Approach is to buy low and sell high. While that's not new advice, Grace contends that most people are so blinded by greed and fear that they fail to follow through; in fact, they often do the opposite. Following the Phoenix Approach will get investors to buy when things look the worst and sell when things look the best.

Grace describes three value determination approaches. The first subscribes to Dreman's low P/E strategy to determine relative value.

Based on this approach, it would be wise to purchase stocks which possess below-average P/Es in combination with above-average yields.

Second, asset valuation determines a company's value by what it owns, using measurements such as cash value per share, working capital per share, and stated book value per share. While asset valuation can highlight potentially undervalued situations, Grace advises using it only in conjunction with other value measurements.

Third, the appraisal valuation method prices a stock by comparing its estimated future income and appreciation to less risky alternative investments.

Checklists for the novice, intermediate, and advanced investors help guide the contrarian in building a Phoenix portfolio. For example, the novice instructions include marking a universe of all common stocks with P/Es of 7 or less in the financial pages. Next, delete any stocks from that listing which have yields of 5 percent or less.

Next, cross off any utility companies in the list of remaining stocks since utility stock prices are often determined by interest rates and are not usually contrarian candidates. The balance of companies should provide a manageable list for further evaluation.

With an emphasis on discovering depressed securities, stocks selling near the low end of their 52-week trading range should prove to be the leading candidates.

Now take the amount of money you have available to invest and purchase equal dollar amounts of five of the remaining stocks, making sure to diversify your portfolio by purchasing stocks in five different industries.

Grace then advises pruning the Phoenix portfolio every six months, selling off those stocks which no longer fit the 7/5 rule (P/E of 7 or less, yield of 5 or more), and replacing them with ones that fit the profile. Even if a stock takes off, Grace says to stick with your strategy and sell it at the six-month interval once it no longer meets the Phoenix criteria.

One final note, the 7/5 rule can be adjusted to take into account market conditions. At one time it may change to a 5/8 rule, while in another market environment it may move to a 10/4 rule.

## THE VALUE LINE RANKING SYSTEM

One of the most widely read stock ranking systems, *The Value Line Investment Survey* (Value Line Publishing, Inc.) enjoys the prestige of beating the market over extended time periods. Its first attempts at ratings appeared in a 1937 book of charts, *The Value Line Ratings*. This became the basis for the popular investment subscription service noted above.

While undergoing several refinements since 1937, the Value Line Ranking System values stocks based on the analysis of several variables, including price and earnings momentum, relative price strength, price stability, probable price performance, company financial strength, and earnings projections. The result: timeliness and safety rankings from one to five, with one being the highest ranking.

From 1965 through 1990, Group one timeliness rankings (without allowing for changes in rank) gained 2,890 percent versus a gain of 1,488 percent for Group two timeliness rankings. In comparison with market averages during that same time, the Dow Jones Industrials Average gained 188 percent and the New York Stock Exchange Composite gained 278 percent. The Value Line record is even more impressive with the weekly changes in rank factored into the returns. In this case, the Group one timeliness rankings gained a whopping 15,641 percent, while Group two timeliness rankings earned 1,334 percent. In both scenarios, the bottom two timeliness rankings far underperformed the other groups, with Group five turning in a negative performance for the 1965–1990 time period.

Value Line recommends concentrating in stocks ranked one or two for expectations of superior year-ahead price performance within the level of risk you wish to assume. It also stresses paying attention to risk reduction through the use of diversification, choosing at least six different industries in which to invest.

## WHITBECK-KISOR MODEL

The Whitbeck-Kisor Model uses projected average annual earnings per share long-term growth, a risk factor, and an expected dividend payout ratio to establish a theoretical price/earnings ratio for stocks for use in comparison for relative attractiveness.

The model first appeared in the May/June 1963 issue of *Financial Analysts Journal* in the article, "A New Tool in Investment Decision Making" by Volkert Whitbeck and Manown Kisor.

In contrast to prior P/E valuation analysis, Whitbeck and Kisor used normalized earnings figures to represent forecasts of earnings during the middle of the business cycles, thereby eliminating cyclical fluctuations.

While Dreman and others seek to ferret out undervalued situations using low P/Es, the Whitbeck-Kisor Model searches for stocks with an actual P/E ratio lower than that calculated by the model based on the company's rate of growth, level of risk (determined by the anticipated standard deviation of a company's expected earnings around its trend), and anticipated dividend payout.

Whitbeck and Kisor considered a stock undervalued or overvalued if its theoretical P/E calculation varied from the actual P/E by 15 percent or more.

David Ahlers later refined the Whitbeck-Kisor Model (called The Ahlers Model) to make the formula multiplicative rather than additive. In addition, the new model reformulated the independent variables using dividend yield instead of dividend payout, substituting the measure of risk as the coefficient of variation instead of the standard deviation, and using the growth in normalized earnings.

## THE EARNINGS REVISION EFFECT

What is the impact of upward earnings revisions and actual earnings coming in higher than projected earnings on future stock price performance? This question was investigated by several investment research studies during the 1980s.

A study by Malcolm Richards and John Martin tracked the price performance of stocks with a minimum 10 percent revision in earnings estimates, either upward or downward. It found that stocks with 10 percent or larger upward revisions earned an excess positive return of 9 percent over the next 12 months. Likewise, excess negative returns of 2 percent after 6 months followed downward earnings estimate revisions over 10 percent or more. Later on, the excess negative returns disappeared.

Follow-on research by D. Givoly and J. Lakonishok confirmed the findings by Richards and Martin and generated a trading rule for taking advantage of large upward earnings revisions.

According to the Givoly and Lakonishok rule, investors should purchase stock at the end of a month in which a 10 percent or larger upward revision occurs and sell stock at the end of a month in which a 10 percent or greater downward revision occurs. Employing this rule should allow investors to earn above-average annual returns in the 15–30 percent range.

## TUCCILLE DYNAMIC INVESTING STRATEGY

In his book, *Dynamic Investing: The System for Automatic Profits No Matter Which Way The Market Goes* (New American Library, 1981), Jerome Tuccille cites new economic factors that have altered the way investors must approach the market and stock picking.

According to Tuccille, investors can no longer expect inflation to remain below 10 percent: we have entered a new era of interest rate levels, conservative investments have vanished, the bond and fixed income security markets have been irreparably damaged, stock market swings have gotten choppier with shorter and shorter cycles, and investors are being forced into becoming traders.

While many of the factors underlying Tuccille's Dynamic Investing Strategy have changed since the early 1980s, some remain, while others can undoubtedly return again. Due to increased market turbulence, Tuccille developed his investment program with the following rules:

◆ Never buy stocks when the yields on risk-free, short-term instruments are higher than 12 or 13 percent.

◆ The best time to buy stocks is when the Dow Jones Industrial Average is under 800 (as originally presented and revised as required).

◆ Stick to household name stocks paying good dividends and selling for under 6 times earnings.

◆ Sell off large portions of stock as it advances in a market rally.

## THE S/B (Sell/Buy) STOCK MARKET RATIO STRATEGY

In 1988, Edwin A. Buck, publisher of Vickers Weekly Insider Report released his book, *The S/B Stock Market Ratio: Profiting from Legal Insider Trading* (Simon & Schuster, Inc.) exploring how the S/B ratio of inside traders can deliver important information for developing and profiting from a S/B Stock Market Ratio investment strategy.

Buck originally developed the S/B ratio in 1971. It is calculated by dividing the number of insider sell decisions by the number of insider buy decisions. Therefore, if there were 75 insider sales transactions and 25 insider buy transactions during a given period, the S/B ratio would be 3.0 The formula disregards sales price, number of shares, and other factors. It concentrates on the insider's investment decision to buy or sell.

According to Buck, an insider buys stock in his or her own company on the open market with only one thing in mind: it's the most attractive investment available. Insider sales, on the other hand, derive from a variety of reasons, including generating cash to cover a new home purchase or upcoming college expenses.

Buck considers a 2.5 S/B ratio normal. The higher the ratio, the more sales are outpacing the buys and the more bearish the sentiment of insiders and vice versa for lower ratios. He contends that the S/B ratio tracks the intensity of insider buying and selling and can predict the market.

As proof, Buck analyzed the 18 times the S/B ratio dropped below 2.0 between 1971 and 1987. In 16 of those occurrences, the Dow Jones Industrial Average followed with a rally averaging a gain of 190 points over an average 6.4 months.

While insiders appear prophetic in their ability to call upside movements based on the S/B ratio, they often sell too early based on the historical evidence.

Basic analysis rules on insider buys include the following: additional purchases by insiders confirm the wise decision of his or her previous buys, a new purchase consisting of a high percentage of his or her former holdings is very bullish, when all officers of a company are purchasing there is probably good reason for them to view the stock positively, when an insider buys in a weak market it's a bullish sign because he or she is discounting the possibility that the stock can be obtained at a better price by waiting, and insider reversals signal a change in the wind.

Insider sales analysis takes into account the number of trades by an insider, the percentage of holdings sold, the number of officers selling, insider reversals, and market direction. An insider selling into a rising market does not believe the market will bail him or her out. Also pay attention to the direction of other industry companies. An insider selling his or her company stock when the stocks of competitors are rising has negative implications for the performance of the company.

## GROWTH STOCK INVESTING STRATEGY

This strategy contends that there are no excess returns to be gained from investing in the tried and true 'Blue Chip' stocks representative of the Dow Jones Industrial Average and the S & P 500. The big profits in the stock market rest in ferreting out the next IBM.

For example, Cisco Systems, Inc., now the leading supplier of high-performance internetworking products for linking computer system networks, traded at $4 1/2 per share shortly after going public in 1990 (adjusted for 2-for-1 stock splits in both 1991 and 1992. At the time, Cisco Systems generated less than $30 million in annual revenues. In 1992, the innovative company looks to reach $325 million in revenues and earn around $1.25 per share.

Alert emerging growth investors who discovered Cisco Systems in its formative years and had the conviction to see its tremendous prospects, even with huge competitors such as IBM and NEC Corporation, earned substantially higher returns than the market averages. From a low of $4 1/2 per share in 1990, the market price of Cisco Systems stock soared to $52 per share in 1992.

Growth stocks and their subset, emerging growth stocks, are well-managed companies operating in industries where earnings and dividends are expected to grow faster than inflation and the overall economy. They are expected to maintain their exceptional growth momentum through economic retractions as well as during economic prosperity.

Typically, growth stocks are not located in the traditional smokestack industries but in new and upcoming fields, such as computers, telecommunications, health care, and biotechnology.

Major characteristics of growth stocks include higher price/earnings ratios than the market average, substantial potential for above-average, long-term price appreciation, price volatility and conservation of capital to fuel growth, therefore little or no dividend payouts in the early years.

For the smaller, emerging growth stocks, price volatility can be even more pronounced due to small capitalization, which makes their shares less liquid; there may be a shortage of available financial and operational information by which to properly judge the company's merits or prospects; investor sentiment swings for large versus small company investments can cause the market price of emerging growth stocks to drop substantially despite rising revenues and earnings and the typical pattern of earnings gains interruptions due to high research and development and expansion expenses can cause investors to flee the stock.

James W. Broadfoot III in his book, *Investing in Emerging Growth Stocks: Making Money With Tomorrow's Blue Chips* (John Wiley & Sons, 1989) spells out how to understand emerging growth stock investing and learn how to pick the right emerging growth stocks for above average returns.

Obviously, the higher returns associated with emerging growth investments also carry with them a higher degree of risk. That's why Broadfoot stresses that investors planning to enter this brand of investing must have a stomach for risk, financial staying power since emerging growth stocks go through cycles of poor performance, and the ability to make a sufficient commitment of time and effort.

According to Broadfoot, the New Horizons Fund's P/E relative to that of the S & P 500 works as an excellent indicator, signalling whether or not investors should enter the emerging growth arena. The T. Rowe Price Associates, Inc. New Horizons Fund has been used as a barometer of the emerging growth market. Historically, a New Horizons' relative P/E of 1.15 times (in other words, a 15 percent premium to the market) or lower meant investors could make money with emerging growth stocks.

As a guideline, Broadfoot suggests holding no cash when the New Horizons relative P/E falls below 1.15 times and gradually cutting back your exposure to stocks as the relative P/E rises. By the time the relative P/E hits 2.0 times, your stock holdings should be at a minimum and your cash positions high.

Emerging growth stock screening standards set forth by Broadfoot include the following:

◆ Avoid companies with two down earning years in the past five

◆ Choose companies with a minimum average 20 percent revenue and earnings growth

◆ Avoid any firm with return on average equity below 13 percent

◆ Avoid firms with debt in excess of 30 percent of total capital

If the firm passes the above tests, consider the growth prospects of the industry (including the degree of industry fragmentation), the level of competition, and the quality of management.

Broadfoot warns about stumbling blocks to the company's success and higher stock prices. A lack of visibility, lengthening sales cycles, and new product dependence can each work to short-circuit the company's potential. In addition, too-rapid growth can wreak havoc with financial and operational controls, causing the company to stumble.

As a warning, Broadfoot says that when emerging growth companies run into trouble, such as a significant earnings shortfall, sell as fast as possible and ask questions later.

Finally, be patient. Emerging growth investing profits don't occur overnight. When you do hit upon a winner, ride it for all its worth; you need the exceptional gains from your winners to make up for the mistakes that come with the emerging growth investing territory.

## THE LOW-SKEWNESS EFFECT

At times, growth stocks fail to deliver the price performance expected of them over the long term. One of the reasons for this market underperformance has been attributed to the attractiveness of these stocks to speculators. In their rush to establish positions in these promising companies, speculators push the market price into overpriced levels, trading the opportunity high, long-term returns for the chance to make a huge, quick profit. The occurrence of this underperformance has been called the "long-shot factor."

In efforts to help investors avoid getting blindsided by the long-shot factor, John S. Howe and William L. Beedles researched attributes of growth companies minimally affected by it. Their resulting analysis found that companies with total assets of at least $80 million in book value and a stockholder's equity/ total assets ratio of at least .60 outperformed the market in their test period of 1962–1980 by an average of 6.5 percent annually.

Analysis of the research appeared in a Winter 1984 article in *Journal of Portfolio Management* by Howe and Beedles. A potential explanation for the excess returns lies in the degree of skewness (bias) toward achieving a higher return. In other words, the higher the skewness value, the greater the possibility of that stock achieving substantial gains in the future.

However, Howe and Beedles found that the stocks outperforming the market in the long-term had a significantly smaller skewness factor.

## SUPERPERFORMANCE STOCKS

A unique twist in investing strategy is presented by Richard S. Love in his book, *Super-Performance Stocks: An Investment Strategy for the Individual Investor Based on the 4-Year Political Cycle* (Prentice-Hall, Inc., 1977).

Love contends that the best stock market gains are made as stocks rebound from the lows of four-year cycles. He traces a number of superperformance phases, which range in length from three months to 63 months.

His research shows that most superperformance stocks are small companies with capitalization of less than five million shares outstanding. Other superperformance characteristics include rapidly increasing earnings, low price/earnings ratios, and a product or service that promises strong future growth.

Love recommends searching for stocks with high past price volatility, a precursor of high volatility. A volatile stock's price rises more in bull markets than the price of the average stock. Rebounding stocks offer the best opportunity for large price gains. With that in mind, Love looks for oversold stocks which experienced sharp declines prior to the market rebound.

Other clues to put the investor on the track of the next super-performer include the discovery of new earning power, such as new product introductions or a change in management; changes such as technological changes or natural resource discoveries that spell opportunity; and expandable price/earnings ratios.

## THE LAST WAVE

Robert Czeschin takes the political scenario one step further in his book, *The Last Wave* (Agora Books, 1988). According to Czeschin, we saw the end of last great wave of investment prosperity with the October 1987 crash. The crash signaled the onset of a decade of extreme risk.

Czeschin helps the reader prepare for the consequences of political and economic upheaval, including discussion of a number of possible scenarios such as the impact of Japan's rearmament, the devastating effect a crash of the Japanese stock market could have on the United States, potential oil-related conflicts, the impact of the banking crisis, and how to avoid being caught up in the carnage of the approaching debacle in mutual funds.

He identifies five major threats lurking to devastate mutual fund profits and points to the effects in the wake of the Crash of 1929—when 50 percent of investment companies went out of business—as evidence it can happen. First, funds still find ways to leverage their returns through the use of margin and speculative futures and options.

Second, record numbers of new mutual funds hint of market tops as evidenced by previous new fund surges prior to 1929 and 1987. Third, since open-end mutual funds comprise such a large segment of the market, they cannot escape a sudden wave of selling. Forced liquidations through massive redemptions can send stock prices spiralling downward even further, significantly slashing funds' net asset values. Fourth, the passion for short-term performance often short circuits long-term investment decision making, setting the funds up for a tumble in the future. Fifth, misleading advertising and outright mutual fund industry fraud continue to occur despite efforts by the Securities and Exchange Commission.

Survival tactics for "riding the last wave" and the coming dependence of America on foreign oil and foreign capital include purchasing oil and airline stocks whenever the price of oil causes either group to fall out of favor. Trading oil and airline stock in countries whose currencies are petrosensitive adds another degree of sophistication to the strategy.

Purchasing foreign securities represents another survival strategy. In this case, Czeschin recommends investigating attractive ADRs (American Depository Receipts). Other suggestions include purchases of precious metals and stakes in Hong Kong and Singapore/Malaysia companies or mutual funds.

## LOWRY'S ECLIPSE INVESTING METHOD

Eclipse investing consists of purchasing stocks during the market's gloomiest days and selling when the market regains confidence and moves into the overconfidence phase of bull markets.

One of the more well-known eclipse investing methods derives from the Lowry's Reports (published by Lowry's Reports, Inc.). In order to determine the extent of buying and selling pressure, Lowry's measured both the volume of shares traded daily and the total amount of gains and losses from those trades. It then used a formula to calculate a buy or sell signal.

The Lowry analysis technique purports to predict the direction of future market moves. While the prediction method may suffer from occasional calling of market moves that never came to pass, it claims to have predicted major market moves in their early stages.

Mutual fund investors were encouraged to purchase growth or aggressive growth mutual funds when Lowry's gave a buy signal and to switch to money market mutual funds when Lowry's gave a sell signal.

A comparison of returns for the 15-year period from January 1, 1968 through February 29, 1984, shows the Lowry's Eclipse Investing Method earning an annualized compounded return of 14.5 percent versus only 6.9 percent for the S & P 500 and 7.6 percent for a hypothetical buy/hold strategy of 21 mutual funds.

## AVERAGING STRATEGIES

One of the most popular investing strategies for the individual investor consists of dollar cost averaging. The practice is relatively simple to employ, as long as you have the discipline to make regular investments no matter where the market has been or appears to be headed.

Simply stated, dollar cost averaging involves the investment of a specific amount of money at regular intervals. The method eliminates the uncertainty of timing the market correctly and missing profit opportunities. In addition, dollar cost averaging delivers an average lower cost per share. During bear markets, as prices drop, more shares are purchased for the same amount of dollar investment. In bull markets with high prices, relatively fewer shares are purchased, thus helping to prevent a major wrong purchase decision. In this way, market ups and down are turned to your advantage.

Most dollar cost averaging strategies recommend reinvesting any dividends and capital gains immediately in order to keep compounding working in your favor.

The keys to dollar cost averaging are a long-term investment horizon and the discipline to make regular contributions. Benefits come from a lower average cost, compounding, and the removal of guesswork from stock purchases.

See Table 5-1 Dollar Cost Averaging for an illustration of how it works. As shown in the chart, the dollar cost average price per share totals $15.00 versus $16.25 for the average share price.

## Table 5-1
## Dollar Cost Averaging

| | Net Amount Invested | Quarter | Share Price | Shares Acquired |
|---|---|---|---|---|
| | $300 | 1 | $20 | 15 |
| | $300 | 2 | $10 | 30 |
| | $300 | 3 | $15 | 20 |
| | $300 | 4 | $20 | 15 |
| Total | $1,200 | Full Year | $65 | 80 |

Average Share Cost:    $15.00 ($1200÷80)
Average Share Price:   $16.25 ($65÷4)

Michael E. Edleson, a Harvard professor, released a new version of averaging strategy which he claims improves on the returns offered by dollar cost averaging. In his book, *Value Averaging* (International Publishing Press, 1992), Edleson explains value averaging helps the investor avoid buying high and selling low. In contrast to dollar cost averaging, which regularly invests a fixed sum of money at regular intervals, value averaging goes one step further. In addition to buying low, you sell when the markets soar.

Here's how it works. You invest an amount required to increase the value of your total account by a fixed amount. Conversely, in strong bull markets, your account value would rise above the desired total and you would sell shares.

For example, assume you desire to raise the value of your investment account by $1,000 each quarter through a combination of additional contributions and increased market values. Your first value averaging purchase results in 50 shares of a stock at a price of $20 per share. In the next quarter, the market price rises to $22 per share. Your account is now worth $1,100 and your required investment would be $900 for 45.45 additional shares.

The market surges, and the price per share jumps to $32.00, making your total account value $3,154.40 (95.45 x $32). Instead of purchasing shares this quarter, you would sell enough shares to get your account down to the desired $3,000 value level.

Value averaging gets you to buy more shares when the price drops exceptionally low and forces you to take your gains as the prices rise sharply.

Downsides include possible excessive transaction costs and the task of periodically calculating your account value in order to decide what to invest or sell. The procedure would work more easily with mutual funds than with individual stock purchases or sales due to the probability of odd-lot and fractional shares purchases.

## THE INVESTMENT CLUB ADVANTAGE

No discussion of dollar cost averaging would be complete without a mention of investment clubs. According to the National Association of Investment Clubs (NAIC) in Royal Oak, Michigan nearly 62 percent of its member clubs have outperformed the total return of the S & P 500 over their clubs' lifetimes, an average of nearly 10 years.

There are four major tenets of successful investing espoused by the NAIC:

1. Invest a set sum of money in common stocks, regardless of market conditions (the dollar cost averaging approach). This forces discipline and a constant analysis of what stocks are undervalued.

2. Buy growth stocks, companies whose sales are increasing at a faster rate than for the industry in general. Prospects for continued above-average growth should be good.

3. Reinvest dividends and capital gains immediately. Your money grows faster if earnings are reinvested—the miracle of compounding.

4. Diversify. Invest in different fields to spread risk.

An obvious advantage of investment clubs lies in its members. Besides pooling their financial resources to purchase stock, investment club members also bring to the table a rich diversity of investment experience. In addition, consensus often helps prevent rash investment decision making. The opportunity to discuss and debate individual proposed purchases and sales provides a forum for thorough investigation before the purchase.

Some clubs also sponsor investment seminars or invite investment specialists to talk to the group, greatly expanding the depth of investment information and resources available for decision making.

## SUCCEEDING IN DRIPS

DRIPS (dividend reinvestment plans) provide another way to enhance investment returns through compounding. Other advantages include avoiding the broker's commission charges on dividend reinvestments, which can be substantial for small lot purchases. Typically, companies absorb the transaction costs of purchasing company shares for plan members. Some companies even allow the sale of company stock through the DRIP program, thereby allowing the investor to escape commissions on both ends of the trade.

Another benefit for investors who want to accumulate shares in excess of that available through dividend reinvestment is that most plans permit additional purchases of company stock within minimum and maximum dollar ranges at specific dates. Some companies even provide price breaks on their stock, offering it at a discount to market value. This allows investors to lock in an immediate gain.

The ease at which dividends can be reinvested provides built-in discipline to grow a financial nest egg. Once the minimal paperwork is out of the way, the stock portfolio grows automatically. To illustrate the benefits of letting your dividends compound through a DRIP, consider the following example. A stock yielding 10 percent annually would return your original investment after 10 years. However, if you reinvested the dividends and allowed them to compound at the same rate, it would now only take seven years and three months to pay back your original investment.

According to the Laurel, Maryland based Evergreen Enterprises, publisher of the ninth edition of the *Directory of Companies Offering Dividend Reinvestment Plans*, around 85 percent of dividend reinvestment plans permit owners of their common stock to purchase additional shares over and above dividend reinvestments, usually in the $25 to $5,000 range per quarter. The directory provides a concise description of each plan. Overall, there are some 1,000 companies that have DRIPs for the benefit of their shareholders.

Other factors that should be considered before signing up for a DRIP are whether or not you need the dividend cash flow to help meet current living expenses and the tax considerations (cash dividends are taxable in the current year even though reinvested).

Another excellent information source on DRIPs is Standard & Poor's updated *Directory of Dividend Reinvestment Plans*, which not only includes DRIP information but also includes a listing of companies that allow plan members to purchase stock directly, bypassing the retail broker, and a listing of DRIPs where $1,000 invested over a 10-year period grew to $10,000 or more.

# 6

# Quantitative, Time and Event Factors

====================

This final chapter of the book details some of the classic quantitative, time-based, and event-related investment strategies that have developed over the years. As mentioned in the preface, a number of the topics covered in this roundup of investment strategies and predictors could rationally be discussed in more than one chapter. The book is intended to be read as a whole; refer to other sections when the need dictates, to help refresh your memory and build your own set of successful predictors and strategies.

## QUANTITATIVE TECHNIQUES

Investors use a number of quantitative techniques to gain a better understanding of market movements, stock relationships, etc. In addition, formulas aid the interpretation of complex market and individual stock information by breaking down significant data into numbers which can be represented on charts, more clearly illustrating what is happening.

Both fundamental and technical market strategists put quantitative techniques to use in order to fine tune their predictive efforts. While most people prefer to start at the beginning, or alpha, I opt to begin this section with beta since it is more well-known and followed by the investment community.

### Beta

Beta is a measure of the price volatility of a specific stock in comparison to the overall market. Given that the S & P 500 has a beta of one, a more volatile stock would have a beta greater than one and would rise and decline faster than the S & P 500. Likewise, stocks with betas under one would rise or decline slower in relation to the S & P 500.

Many investors consider beta to be an accurate measurement of the level of risk (and opportunity) inherent in a particular stock due to its degree of volatility. The riskiness of your overall portfolio is determined by the mix of stocks you own and the betas associated with those stocks.

Beta is defined as the expected market return on a security divided by the return on a market index such as the S & P 500. For example, if investors expect XYZ stock to return 11 percent and the overall market to return 10 percent, XYZ would have a beta of 1.1. On the other hand if, XYZ's expected return was only 9 percent, then its beta would calculate out to .9.

If the market were to move 15 percent, a security with a beta of .9 would be expected to move only 90 percent of that amount or 13.5 percent (15 x .9), while a security with a beta of 1.1 would be expected to move 110 percent of the market move or 16.5 percent (15 x 1.1) in the same direction.

For years, investors used betas to construct portfolios consistent with their individual investment objectives and risk parameters in order to earn higher returns. However, a 1992 investment research report by Eugene Fama and Kenneth French, both professors at the

University of Chicago, casts doubt on the ability of the use of beta to deliver higher returns.

Fama and French measured the performance of thousands of stocks over a period of 50 years and found that there is no link between risk, as defined by beta, and long-term performance. One analyst says that a potential message coming out of the Fama/French research report is that long-term average returns are inversely correlated with price/book ratios and the size of a stock's market capitalization.

The *Value Line Investment Survey* uses its own version of beta in its stock analysis efforts. It derives the Value Line Beta from a regression analysis technique using weekly price changes of a stock and weekly percent changes in the New York Stock Exchange Composite Index over the past five years.

The basic premise is that most investors act rationally and will accept greater risk only with an expectation of greater returns. Therefore, high beta stocks should earn higher returns in rising markets and lower returns in declining markets.

While Value Line acknowledges the challenges against the use of beta, it contends that it can still be a useful analytical tool when used in context with a clearly defined advancing or declining market.

The beta debate will roar on for years. As with any investment technique or predictor, it has its ardent proponents and vehement detractors. Investigate for yourself and use whatever techniques, predictors, strategies, and theories that help enhance your investment return.

### Alpha

Moving backwards from beta to alpha, we find that while beta refers to the slope of the regression line (the amount of vertical movement per unit of horizontal movement or, in other words, the degree of volatility), alpha refers to the point where the line crosses the vertical axis and zero on the horizontal axis (representing the amount of return produced by a stock independent of any relationship to the return of the market).

Alphas can be positive, negative or zero. While negative betas (where a stock rises as the market falls or vice versa) can occur, they're not very common.

Putting the alpha and beta together, an investor can determine the anticipated average return for a stock. For example, assume that XYZ's alpha is 1 percent and its beta is 1.25 percent. Now if the market's expected return for a given month equals 2 percent, the most probable return on XYZ stock for that month will calculate out to 3.5 percent.

The 3.5 percent return was derived as follows: since XYZ stock sports a beta of 1.25, its should earn 1.25 times the expected market return or 2.5 percent (2.0 x 1.25). On top of the beta factor, XYZ also earns an additional return independent of its relationship to the market (alpha) of 1 percent. Therefore, the total expected return for XYZ is 3.5 percent (2.5 + 1.0).

While the alphas and betas of individual stocks may not closely correlate with their actual performance, proponents of the theory contend that a diversified portfolio will move the actual returns more closely in line with the expected returns because the individual positive and negative alphas work to offset each other, and any deviations from betas also tend to average out.

### Markowitz Expected Return-Variance Model

Harry Markowitz first introduced mathematics into the realm of risk reduction analysis in his book, *Portfolio Selection* (Wiley, 1959).

He attacked the process of portfolio selection through three processes: estimating the probability of future stock performance, analyzing those estimates to determine an efficient set of portfolios, and choosing the portfolios from the available set that promise to meet the investor's goal and risk parameters best. In this way, the Markowitz Model sought to find the optimal portfolio diversification by measuring the return and variance of the portfolio.

Once the return and variances were measured for distinct portfolios, the results were used for comparisons with the results of other portfolios, in the search for alternative risk/return tradeoffs and the ultimate portfolio or set of portfolios to meet the investor's specific investment goals.

Under this model, for each level of expected return, there exists one optimum portfolio that delivers the level of expected return with the least variance or risk. Any other portfolio, meeting the investor's investment goals will have associated with it a higher degree of variance.

## Capital Market Equilibrium Theory (CMT)

The CMT is centered around developing a sufficiently diversified investment portfolio to yield the same return and assume the same risks as the market portfolio (market index), drawing them into equilibrium.

Various versions of efficient portfolio diversification exist, but each takes into account the expected return and some measure of risk associated with the mix of securities in the portfolio. Most of these formulas engage in an analysis of alpha and beta as discussed above, typically ignoring the variables of security selection and investment timing.

Another problem with CMT analysis stems from its propensity to evaluate investment decision making under certain risk conditions instead of performing the analysis under conditions of uncertainty. While the market obviously contains elements of risk, these risks are encountered within an uncertain environment.

## Capital-Asset Pricing Model (CAPM)

Professors William Sharpe and John Lintner took the diversification model one step further in the 1960s, attempting to focus on the security risks which can be eliminated. The resulting CAPM describes the behavior of security returns in efficient markets.

Despite Sharpe and Lintner having employed a number of assumptions, such as ignoring transaction costs and income tax considerations in the construction of their CAPM Model, the model has fairly accurately portrayed actual market behavior over the years.

CAPM rests on the premise that stock risk consists of two distinct parts: market risk and non-market risk. Investors strive to build investment portfolios that work to eliminate the non-market risks by selecting an appropriate mix of stocks that deliver the desired expected returns.

With this optimal non-market risk elimination in place, the CAPM measures market risk, specifically beta. According to CAPM theory, a security is undervalued if its expected return consistently come in below its actual return. See Figure 6-1, CAPM Risk/Return Relationship. On the chart, the risk-free interest rate represents the ideal investment without risk. While every investment involves a degree of risk, the interest rate on 90-day U.S. Treasury Bills is used to simulate the ideal risk-free investment return.

The basis formula for CAPM is:

Rate of Return = Risk-free Rate + Beta (Market Return Risk-free Rate)

### Dividend Discount Model

The basic assumption of the dividend discount model is that the value of a stock stems from the present value of future cash dividend payouts.

The present value of a stock is derived from the Dividend Discount Model as follows:

$$PV = \frac{(1-G)D}{1+R} + \frac{(1+G)^2 D}{(1+R)^2} + \ldots + \frac{(1+G)^n D}{(1+R)^n}$$

where: $G$ = growth rate of dividends
$R$ = discount rate
$D$ = current dividend rate

Of course, the estimation of any future event such as the dividend growth rate and discount rate are "best guesses" based on available information. Different assumptions by different investors can yield drastically different present valuations for a company's stock.

Some investors modify the dividend discount model to use earnings growth estimates in the place of dividend growth forecasts.

**Figure 6-1**
**CAPM Risk/Return Relationship**

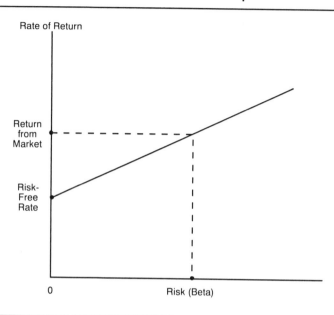

## Black-Scholes Pricing Formula

On the options front, the Black-Scholes mathematical model for pricing options has been acclaimed as an efficient pricing mechanism as well as damned as a contributor to the October 1987 stock market crash.

Developed by Fisher Black and Myron Scholes in 1973, the Black-Scholes Pricing Formula brought option pricing strategies out of the investment world dark ages. Instead of trying to factor in investor risk attitudes and expectations of future market performance, Black and Scholes concentrated on pricing options based on their three main determinants: stock price, interest rates, and stock price volatility.

The Black-Scholes formula involves complicated mathematics, which can be found in more detailed treatments of the subject. Suffice it to say, the result of Black-Scholes calculations end with trading strategies which advise purchasing the option when the market price is less than the formula price; writing an option when the market price is greater than the formula price; and hedging the option against the stock, using a hedge ratio calculation.

Refinements to the Black-Scholes model by the originators and other have appeared over the years, but the basic premise remains the same.

## TIME-BASED PREDICTORS

In addition to the Presidential Theory discussed in Chapter 1, a number of other time-related theories have sprung up over the years. For an in-depth discussion of many time-based theories, I recommend that you seek out a current edition of *Stock Trader's Almanac* (Old Tappan, New Jersey: The Hirsch Organization, Inc.)

### Best Days of the Week

The *Stock Trader's Almanac* section, "Don't Sell Stock on Monday" shows that from 1953 through 1990, the middle of the week seems to be the clear winner with a 1736.01 change in the Dow versus 1,279.93 for Friday, the next closest contender. While Wednesdays and Fridays had the same number of days with gains, Wednesdays turned in a better Dow performance.

As the section's title indicates, Monday proved to be a disastrous day for stocks. While the Dow Jones Industrial Average gained over 2,341 points during that time frame, Mondays turned in a horrible performance, losing 1,896.96. In fact, it was the only day of the week with a loss over the whole period.

### Best Months of the Year

Yale Hirsch also computed records for the best months of the year from data stretching from January 1950 through April 1991. According to his statistics, November ranks number one in performance, with an average 1.7 percent gain in the S & P 500 followed closely by December and January with average rises of 1.6 percent. On the downside, September took the dubious honors, dropping an average 0.7 percent. The only other down month was May with an average negative 0.1 percent performance.

## Best Pre-Holiday Trading Days of the Year

In his classic book, *Behavior of Prices on Wall Street*, Arthur Merrill of Merrill Analysis, Inc. in Haverford, Pennsylvania, studied stock market performance of the trading days prior to holidays. Since then, John McGinley, who took over the position of editor of *Technical Trends* (Wilton, Connecticut) from Merrill, has been keeping the pre-holiday data updated.

Based on stock market information dating back to 1897, McGinley points out that the days before Labor Day earn the honor of delivering price rises with an impressive track record of increases over 81 percent of the time.

The trading days before Memorial Day garner the second slot in terms of market performance with advances 76 percent of the time, closely followed by the days before Independence Day (July Fourth) with rises 74 percent of the time.

However, the record for the days before Independence Day has been a bit tarnished as of late. Out of the past 17 years, there's only been an advance six times.

On average, the days before a holiday post gains around 68 percent of the time. That compares very favorably with the typical trading day, which rises only 52 percent of the time.

Norman G. Fosback, author of *Stock Market Logic* (Dearborn Financial Publishing, Inc., latest edition 1991) says an investor can benefit from the pre-holiday phenomenon by factoring this seasonal trend into a long-term investment policy: timing purchases just prior to the commencement of a pre-holiday period and making stock sales just after (remember, long term, not in the same week).

## The January Effect

There's been a lot of controversy over the so-called January Effect. Advocates like Yale Hirsch claim the year's first month has been a faithful barometer of the year's market. On the other extreme, Norman G. Fosback points out what he considers flaws in the January Effect analysis.

As backup, Hirsch's *Stock Trader's Almanac* shows that from 1950 through 1991, an increase in the S & P 500 in January has been followed by an increase in the S & P 500 for the whole year 36 times out of 41, an 87 percent forecasting accuracy rate. Taking it one step further and tying it to the convening of new congresses, January improves to 100 percent accuracy in predicting the course of the year's market.

According to Hirsch, all bear markets were preceded or accompanied by inferior Januarys, and the top Januarys launched the best market years.

For his part, Fosback finds fault with including January results in comparison with the year's performance since it adds a bias that the year will move in the same direction. He also points out that January's forecasting results prior to 1949 have not been quite as stellar, with accurate calls less than half the time for years before 1949.

Fosback maintains that a coin flip on New Year's Eve will deliver as good a chance of being right about the February-to-December market as the January Barometer, plus you'll have your forecast 31 days earlier.

## Summer Rally

Close on the heels of the heated January Effect debate, the Summer Rally also draws its share of controversy. In this case, Hirsch, along with others, plays the naysayer role.

The Summer Rally, first identified decades ago by Ralph Rotnem at Smith Barney, has long been a tradition on Wall Street. According to Wall Street legend, a Summer Rally boosts the Dow

Jones Industrial Average from a May/June low to a new high sometime during the three-month summer period from July through September.

Mark Hulbert, editor of the Washington, D.C.-based *Hulbert Financial Digest* and columnist for *Forbes,* also downplays any Summer Rally influence on the stock market. Hulbert conducted his own Summer Rally research in 1987. Analyzing market trends between June 21 and September 21 (the first and last days of summer), Hulbert computed the difference between the Dow's value on those days for each of the 50 years between 1937 and 1986.

According to Hulbert, summer was no more bullish than any other time of the year. The average percentage change over the three summer months during the 50-year time frame totaled 1.696 percent. The average advance for the Dow for that same time period was 6.2 percent, close to a rate of the 1.696 percent on a quarterly basis.

Looking at it another way, Hulbert also argues that summer months are not "up" months any more than other periods of the year. Despite 33 of the 50 summers in the sample being "up" periods, in fact, 32 of those 50 years were also "up" *years.*

Hulbert also points to a comprehensive study of seasonal stock market patterns by University of Illinois Professor Josef Lakonishok and Cornell University Professor Seymour Smidt as reported in the Winter, 1988 issue of *Review of Financial Studies.* In their research, Lakonishok and Smidt found no evidence of a June through August Summer Rally. They did however find support for other seasonal stock market patterns, including the above mentioned January Effect and pre-holiday activity.

Hirsch notes that despite the lack of evidence for the elusive Summer Rally, he did uncover a ten-day July period (the five trading days before July 4 and the five trading days after July 4) which could constitute a "mid-year rally." During this period, the trading day before July 4th gained an average .32 percent, and the other nine days gained an average 1.14 percent compared to an overall July change of 0.9 percent.

Taking a look at July by itself, Hirsch found that during the 41-year period through 1991, July posted advances during 14 of the first 17 years but only nine times in the last 24 years. The best all-time July performance occurred in 1989, followed by the October Crash. According to Hirsch, great performances in July during bull markets often precede October massacres as evidenced by 1978, 1987, and 1989, or bear markets as in 1973 and 1980.

Turning to August, Hirsh's research shows that although August turned in a bullish performance 80 percent of the time during the first half of the century, since then its record has only been 50 percent. Finally, September stock market action turns in an average lose of 0.7 percent; no Summer Rally evidence here either. In fact, the Dow has only risen four times in the past 22 Septembers.

Now, if you're still looking for a rally within the summer time frame to pin your hat on, consider the last three trading days before Labor Day. As mentioned earlier, the trading days before Labor Day delivered increases over 81 percent of the time. For 18 straight years through 1978, the stock market rose over the three-day period before Labor Day.

However, no stock market phenomenon works forever; since 1978, the pre-Labor Day trading days have failed to produce gains in 7 of the past 13 years.

Other stock market action in Hirsch's *Stock Trader's Almanac* that bears watching are the following:

◆ Excluding 1932 and 1962, the second years of decades possess a modest upward bias

◆ The first half of April outperforms the second half 25 of 37 times

◆ Since 1950, November through April gained 2,937.05 while May through October lost 263.21

◆ A May/June disaster is most likely in Presidential Election Year

◆ When the market gains between New Year's Day and Election Day, the incumbent party usually retains the Presidency

◆ Since 1960, September has been a remarkable reverse barometer with bearish Septembers typically being followed by bullish fourth quarters and vice versa

## EVENT FACTORS

Despite the efficient market theory's contention that all information regarding a company and the business environment in which it operates gets immediately absorbed and reflected in the stock price, a tremendous amount of research has been conducted over the years to determine the effects, if any, of specific events on future stock market prices. The following discussion presents the current body of evidence on a number of these event-related stock market predictors.

### Analyst Recommendations

Every day, investment research analysts across the nation issue a myriad of research reports and buy/sell/hold recommendations. Some investors, both individual and professional, religiously use these reports to structure their investment portfolios and, indeed, to make individual stock purchases and sales.

Other market players, like Donald L. Cassidy, author of *It's Not What Stocks You Buy, It's When You Sell That Counts* (Probus Publishing, 1991) and a closed-end fund research analyst with Lipper Analytical Services, Inc. in Denver, caution to read between the lines when reviewing research reports.

According to Cassidy, the investor must be on the alert for euphemisms for the word *sell*. Often, follow-up reports carry no official opinions or recommendations; however, the tone of the report needs to be considered carefully to ferret out its real significance. If the report is less than glowing, suspect that the analyst is less than impressed with the company's prospects and its stock and really thinks it should be sold.

Cassidy warns that when an analyst does not want to issue a buy recommendation but is prohibited by company policy to issue a sell recommendation, the only remaining option is to hold. He advises considering a hold recommendation a warning sign and says it can, in fact, be interpreted as meaning "do not hold."

Another caution phrase in research analyst reports, "probably a worthwhile long-term holding despite some near-term uncertainties" can be translated into "if you hold for quite awhile, maybe you won't lose money on this stock."

Cassidy advises asking your broker about the exact meaning of his or her firm's recommendation terminology and the range of recommendations. Anything less enthusiastic than the top recommendation choice should be construed as a "shot across the bow" if not an outright damnation and a time to close out your position on that stock or even take a short position.

An early 1980's study by Elton, Gruber and Grossman of New York University on the effect of brokerage firm recommendations on stock prices found that excess returns are obtainable via purchases of stock from recommended lists.

Based on a review of more than 10,000 recommendations per month by over 700 research analysts from 33 brokerage firms during the period March 1981 through November 1983, Elton, Gruber and Grossman found excess returns of 3.37 percent over a 13-month period. (Only companies followed by at least three analysts were included in the study, typically firms with a market capitalization over $50 million.)

It's important to note that the majority of the excess returns took place over the first two months following the recommendation. However, the ability of the stocks to maintain the excess returns over 13 months adds credence to the theory that the analyst research reports can project an accurate portrayal of the firm's value and its potential future stock price.

Table 6-1 reflecting data as presented by Elton, Gruber and Grossman in the Volume 41, 1986 issue of *The Journal of Finance* shows the cumulative excess returns for newly ranked number one stocks in comparison with number three stocks as found in their research study.

**Table 6-1**
**Excess Return of Newly Ranked #1 Stocks**

| Month | Cumulative Excess Return Percentage |
|-------|-------------------------------------|
| 0 | 1.91% |
| 1 | 3.14 |
| 2 | 3.43 |
| 3 | 3.32 |
| 4 | 3.69 |
| 5 | 3.75 |
| 6 | 4.03 |
| 9 | 3.98 |
| 11 | 3.53 |
| 12 | 3.19 |
| 13 | 3.37 |

While their research reflected that above-average returns can be made following the number one ranking recommendations of brokerage firms, Elton, Gruber and Grossman did not find any one brokerage firm that outperformed the research report recommendations of others.

Other studies concluded the following about earnings projections in analyst research reports: current consensus earnings forecasts were already factored into current stock price levels, excess returns can be made by those who can determine which stocks' earnings have been underestimated by analysts, and the most excess returns will be earned by investors able to accurately predict which stocks will experience the largest positive earnings estimate revisions.

If the greatest excess returns can be earned by "outguessing" the research analysts, who make their livings doing this, what are the odds of outwitting the analysts?

David Dreman, chairman of Dreman Value Management, L.P. and author of *The New Contrarian Strategy*, in conjunction with Michael Berry, a professor at James Madison University, undertook a study of the accuracy of analysts' estimates from 1973 through 1990. (This study included only companies with a following of at least six analysts, approximately 800 NYSE and AMEX firms per quarter.)

According to Dreman and Berry's research, the accuracy of analyst's estimates have been less than impressive. In fact, even though the estimates were made less than three months before the release of actual earnings, they were consistently off the mark. The average error over the entire time frame for the nearly 60,000 estimates stood at 40 percent annually.

Instead of getting better over time, the ability of analysts to accurately predict earnings appears to have deteriorated. For example, over the past six years through 1990, the average error rose to 52 percent. The record for the last two years of the study proved even more dramatic with average errors of 57 percent and 65 percent, respectively.

As Dreman indicates, an estimate change on only 10 percent can contribute to major stock movements. Consider the impact of errors of 57 percent in 1989 and 65 percent in 1990.

## Mergers and Takeovers

The underlying economics behind many mergers and takeovers lies in improving the overall return of the remaining company. The proposed merger or takeover may arise for a variety of reasons, including the management of one company considering the other company's assets undervalued, a desire to capture market share quickly, promised operating and financial synergies that will result in lower costs and more efficient operations, an opportunity to acquire new product lines, technologies and/or research and development capabilities, etc.

Of course, all mergers and takeovers don't work out as expected. Some abort after months of effort and huge expenses; others result in the companies incurring substantial expenses due to legal maneuvers and lengthy and hotly contested take-over battles; some fail to deliver the degree of anticipated benefits and still others become an albatross around the neck of the acquiring or merged company, driving down earnings and the firm's stock market price.

What then do announcements of mergers or takeovers portend for investors? A substantial body of research has been dedicated to answering this question. An in-depth study of mergers by Harvard Professor Paul Asquith researched more that 200 successful mergers and 91 failed mergers of target firms traded on the New York Stock Exchange between 1962 and 1976.

Asquith tracked the price performance of both the target firm and the acquiring firm over a period of time stretching from 480 days before the announcement of a merger bid and up to 240 days after the announcement of the final outcome.

As reported in the *Journal of Financial Economics* (Volume 11, 1983), Asquith calculated the excess returns for this period for the different types of firms involved in the proposed merger. Excess return results are illustrated in Table 6-2.

As expected, successful target firms earned an average excess return (16.1%) due to the merger, while failed merger target firms experienced an average negative excess return (–19.6). More surprising, however, both successful (–7.4) and unsuccessful (–15.4) bidders turned in negative excess returns.

Based on this study's results, some investors concentrate on uncovering potential target companies in order to capitalize on that

### Table 6-2
### Excess Returns for Firms Involved in Merger Proposals

| Type of Firm | | Bid Day | Interim Period | Outcome Day | Post-Outcome | Cumulative Change |
|---|---|---|---|---|---|---|
| Success | Target | 6.2% | 8.6% | 1.3% | N/A | 16.1% |
| Unsuc | Target | 7.0 | –11.5 | –6.4 | –8.7 | –19.6 |
| Success | Bidder | 0.2 | –0.6 | 0.2 | –7.2 | –7.4 |
| Unsuc | Bidder | 0.5 | –6.1 | –0.2 | –9.6 | –15.4 |

company's stock price rise in the event the proposed merger succeeds. The study also points out that holders of stock in companies involved in a merger should sell their stock immediately after the merger outcome day since the post-outcome period results in negative excess returns for all firms involved in the merger. Successive research basically confirmed the findings of the Asquith research.

On the hostile takeover front, a research study by University of Rochester Professors Clifford D. Holderness and Dennis P. Sheehan, reported in the *Journal of Financial Economics*, (Volume 9, Spring 1983) found that a strategy of purchasing shares in takeover attempts can prove to be a successful way to earn excess returns.

To illustrate, takeover target firms that successfully reorganized earned an excess return of 13.0 percent from the time of the initial stock purchase announcement to the final event; target firms with unsuccessful reorganizations earned an excess return of 4.1 percent; and takeover target firms that repurchased their own shares earned an excess return of 3.2 percent.

## Corporate Spinoffs

Several new studies have confirmed that corporate spinoffs can present unique investment opportunities for the astute investor to earn excess returns.

As with mergers and takeovers, there's plenty of reasons why companies engage in corporate spinoffs. The proposed spinoff unit may no longer fit into corporate long-range strategical planning; management may believe it's a way to unlock the hidden value of a small corporate unit for its shareholders; management may feel the unit will perform better when unleashed from its corporate bonds and restrictions; and the unit may plain and simple be a dog, dragging down corporate earnings and valuation by the market.

Inefficiencies by the market to properly value spinoff companies provide savvy investors with the opportunity to capitalize on the value/market price imbalance. The undervaluation can come about for several reasons. First of all, spinoffs come to market without a lot of information. Typically buried deep in the corporate structure of ent, they are little understood and attract little research analyst following, at least until they prove their worth.

Second, adverse price pressure results from institutions shedding their spinoff shares early in the game. Sometimes the institutions' investment policies prevent their continuing to hold securities below a certain investment grade or not paying dividends. In other cases, institutional portfolio managers don't want to hold securities they know little about. Either way, the rapid exit of institutions as shareholders of the spinoff company helps to create a negative valuation/stock market price imbalance.

According to a University of Texas study by associate professors Keith C. Brown and Van Harlow, a vice president with Fidelity Management Trust Company in Boston, these outside factors contributed to a significant but temporary negative price pressure as institutional sellers unloaded their holdings.

A Pennsylvania State University study by Cusatis, Miles and Woolridge found an average raw buy-and-hold return in excess of 74 percent for spinoffs over the first three years, with the most favorable excess performance occurring during the first two years after the spinoff.

In addition, the spinoffs' parents also delivered excess raw buy-and-hold returns in excess of 60 percent. A high incidence of takeovers contributed to the higher-than-market returns for both the spinoff companies and their parents.

### Stock Splits

On the surface, nothing is changed in the wake of a stock split—investors still hold the same proportional share of the company after the split as they did before the split.

However, a preponderance of evidence suggests that stock splits can and do enhance a stock's future price performance, given certain conditions.

While no change in the relative capital structure of the firm takes place, changes do occur in investors' perception of the company, which may alert them to previously undervalued prospects for the company's operations and the firm's future stock price level.

A stock split, particularly those accompanied by cash dividend increases, can be looked upon as a strong vote of confidence by the board of directors. A New York Stock Exchange study indicates that firms which have split their shares are 2 1/2 times more likely to increase their cash dividend payout.

Another factor entering the picture lies in the perception that individual investors prefer to purchase 800 shares of a $30 per share stock versus 400 shares of a $60 per share stock even though the investment outlay is the same.

In addition, the added shares and potentially broadened shareholder base may work to decrease the volatility of the firm's per share stock price.

A 1984 study by Grinblatt, Masulis, and Titman concluded that stock prices, on average, react positively to stock split announcements (and dividend announcements) that are not contaminated by other simultaneous announcements, such as earnings releases and mergers announcements.

There's plenty of opportunity to profit from stock splits. According to the New York Stock Exchange Inc.'s *1991 Fact Book*, 107 companies on the New York Stock Exchange split their stocks in that year. See Figure 6-2 Annual Number of Stock Splits and Table 6-3 Listing of 1991 Stock Splits.

To be sure, stock price rises are not automatic after stock splits. Investors need to make an analysis of the future prospects of the firm. Higher prices over the long term tend to generate from the prospects for higher earnings and bigger dividends in the future rather than from the stock split itself.

In addition to the daily financial publications, *Barron's*, Standard & Poor's *The Outlook* and *The Value Line Investment Survey* represent excellent sources of information on stock splits.

### It's in the Stars

Moving from such earthly events as mergers, takeovers, spinoffs and stock splits to a more heavenly topic, the Sunspot Indicator owes its origin to 19th century astronomer Sir William Herschel.

## Figure 6-2
## Annual Number of Stock Splits

| | Less than 25% | 25% to 49% | 50% to 99% | 2-for-1 to 2½-for-1 | 3-for-1 to 3½-for-1 | 4-for-1 | Over 4-for-1 | Total |
|---|---|---|---|---|---|---|---|---|
| 1991 | 18 | 8 | 33 | 45 | 1 | — | 1 | 107 |
| 1990 | 25 | 7 | 19 | 49 | 2 | — | 3 | 105 |
| 1989 | 28 | 9 | 34 | 55 | 2 | 2 | 1 | 142 |
| 1988 | 34 | 11 | 29 | 25 | 4 | 1 | — | 104 |
| 1987 | 36 | 18 | 59 | 118 | 10 | 1 | 2 | 244 |
| 1986 | 43 | 22 | 78 | 118 | 9 | 1 | 1 | 272 |
| 1985 | 40 | 17 | 43 | 60 | 8 | — | — | 165 |
| 1884 | 57 | 12 | 50 | 51 | 6 | 1 | 1 | 178 |
| 1983 | 54 | 21 | 80 | 131 | 12 | — | 2 | 300 |
| 1982 | 61 | 21 | 35 | 28 | — | — | — | 146 |

*Note:* Includes common and preferred issues. Data based on effective dates.

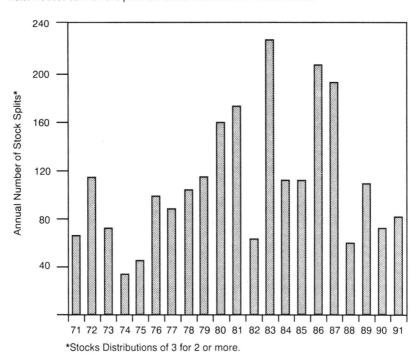

*Stocks Distributions of 3 for 2 or more.

*Source:* NYSE, Inc. 1991 Fact Book

## Table 6-3
## Listing of 1991 Stock Splits

| Company | Symbol | Company | Symbol |
|---|---|---|---|
| **5-for 1** | | | |
| Vornado, Inc. | VNO | | |
| | | | |
| **3-for-1** | | | |
| IMCERA Group, Inc. | IMA | | |
| | | | |
| **2-for-1** | | | |
| American Stores Company | ASC | Logicon, Inc. | LGN |
| Automatic Data Processing Inc. | AUD | Lydall, Inc. | LDL |
| Bausch & Lomb Inc. | BOL | Medtronic, Inc. | MDT |
| Blockbuster Entertainment Corp. | BV | Morgan Stanley Group Inc. | MS |
| Campbell Soup Company | CPB | Nalco Chemical Company | NLC |
| Circus Circus Enterprises, Inc. | CIR | National Medical Enterprises Inc. | NME |
| CML Group, Inc. | CML | Pfizer Inc. | PFE |
| Colgate-Palmolive Company | CL | Philipps-Van Heusen Corporation | PVH |
| Conseco, Inc. | CNC | Questar Corporation | STR |
| Enron Corp. | ENE | Ralston Purina Company | RAL |
| Gap, Inc. | GPS | Rhone-Poulenc Rorer Inc. | RPR |
| General Public Utilities Corp. | GPU | Rite Aid Corporation | RAD |
| Gillette Company | GS | Rubbermaid Inc. | RBD |
| Glaxo Holdings p.l.c. | GLX | Sea Containers Ltd. | SCR |
| Grainger (W.W.), Inc. | GWW | Sherwin-Williams Company | SHW |
| H&R Block Inc. | HRB | Stride Rite Corporation | SRR |
| Hancock Fabrics, Inc. | HKF | Syntex Corporation | SYN |
| House of Fabrics, Inc. | HF | Union Pacific Corporation | UNP |
| International Game Technology | IGT | United States Surgical Corp. | USS |
| Jacobs Engineering Group Inc. | JEC | Universal Corporation | UVV |
| Kellogg Company | K | Value City Department Stores | VCD |
| Liberty Corporation | LC | Walgreen Co. | WAG |
| Loctite Corporation | LOC | Wheelabrator Technologies, Inc. | WTI |

*Source:* NYSE, Inc. 1991 Fact Book

While the 11-year sunspot cycle now purports to predict stock market direction, it originally flowed from Herschel's tying of peaks and valleys in sunspots to climatic changes and the abundance or scarcity of wheat crops. As sunspots peaked, the world's climate improved and an abundance of wheat drove wheat market prices down. Likewise, a decrease in sunspot activity coincided with poor climate resulting in wheat scarcity and higher wheat prices. Peak sunspot activity is now related to a bear market and vice versa.

Not to be outdone, Dr. Arnold Leiber ties phases of the moon and the gravitational power of the moon to human emotions that in turn drive the financial markets.

In order to drive your investment returns to lofty heights, keep your head out of the clouds, your feet on the ground and your eyes on the market indicators, predictors, theories, strategies and foibles that can give you an edge in the competitive investment world. Good Luck.

# Glossary

**Annual Report.** Required by the Securities and Exchange Commission, the report presents a portrayal of the company's operations and financial position. It includes a balance sheet, income statement, statement of cash flows, description of company operations, management discussion of the company's financial condition and operating results, and any events which materially impact the company.

**Asset Play.** A stock investment that value investors find attractive due to asset undervaluation by the market.

**Basis Price.** The cost of an investment used to determine capital gains or losses.

**Bear Market.** A period of time (months or years) during which stock prices decline.

**Bond.** A long-term debt security which obligates the issuer to pay interest and repay the principal. The holder does not have any ownership rights in the issuer.

**Bond Ratio.** The measure of a company's leverage, comparing the firm's debt to total capital.

**Bottom Up Investing.** An investment strategy starting with company fundamentals and then moving to the overall economic and investment environment.

**Call Option.** A contract providing the holder the right to buy the underlying security at a specific price during a specified time period.

**Call Provision.** A provision allowing the security issuer to recall the security before maturity.

**Cash Equivalent.** An asset type with maturities of less than one year.

**Cash Flow.** The flow of funds in and out of an operating business. Normally calculated as net income plus depreciation and other non-cash items.

**Cash Flow/Debt Ratio.** The relationship of free cash flow to total long-term indebtedness. This ratio is helpful in tracking a firm's ability to meet scheduled debt and interest payment requirements.

**Cash Flow/Interest Ratio.** This ratio determines how many times free cash flow will cover fixed interest payments on long-term debt.

**Cash Flow per Share.** Cash flow per share represents the amount earned before deduction for depreciation and other charges not involving the outlay of cash.

**Cash Ratio.** This ratio is used to measure liquidity. It is calculated as the sum of cash and marketable securities divided by current liabilities. It indicates how well a company can meet current liabilities.

**Common and Preferred Cash Flow Coverage Ratios.** These ratios determine how many times annual free cash flow will cover common and preferred cash dividend payments.

**Common Stock Ratio.** The relationship of common stock to total company capitalization.

**Contrarian.** An investor seeking securities out of favor with other investors.

**Convertibles.** A security that is exchangeable into common stock at the option of the holder under specified terms and conditions.

**Current Ratio.** A liquidity ratio calculated by dividing current assets by current liabilities.

**Cyclical.** Industries and companies that advance and decline in relation to the changes in the overall economic environment.

**Debt-to-Equity Ratio.** The relationship of debt to shareholder's equity in a firm's capitalization structure.

**Defensive Investments.** Securities that are less affected by economic retractions, thus offering downside price protection.

**Diversification.** The spreading of investment risk by owning different types of securities, investments in different geographical markets, etc.

**Dollar Cost Averaging.** Investment strategy of investing a fixed amount of money over time to achieve a lower average security purchase price.

**Dow Jones Industrial Average.** Market index consisting of 30 U.S. industrial companies. Used as a measure of market performance.

**Earnings per Share.** Net after tax income divided by the number of outstanding company shares.

**Economic Value.** The economic value of a stock represents the anticipated free cash flow the company will generate over a period of time, discounted by the weighted cost of a company's capital.

**Efficient Market.** A market which instantly takes into account all known financial information and reflects it in the security's price.

**Exercise Price.** The price at which an option of futures contract can be executed. Also known as the striking price.

**Expiration Date.** The last day on which an option or future can be exercised.

**Federal Reserve.** The national banking system, consisting of twelve independent federal reserve banks in Atlanta, Boston, Chicago, Cleveland, Dallas, Kansas City, Minneapolis, New York, Philadelphia, Richmond, St. Louis, and San Francisco.

**Fiscal Year.** The twelve-month accounting period that conforms to the company's natural operating cycle versus the calendar year.

**Freddie Mac.** The nickname of the Federal Home Loan Mortgage Corporation.

**Free Cash Flow.** Free cash flow is determined by calculating operating earnings after taxes and then adding depreciation and other non-cash expenses, less capital expenditures and increases in working capital.

**Free Cash Flow/Earnings Ratio.** The percentage of earnings actually available in cash. It is the percentage of free cash available to company management for investments, acquisitions, plant construction, dividends, etc.

**Fundamental Analysis.** Investment strategy focusing on the intrinsic value of the company as evidenced by a review of the balance sheet, income statement, cash flow, operating performance, etc.

**Gap.** The occurrence of a trading pattern when the price range from one day does not overlap the previous day's price range.

**Growth Investments.** Companies or industries with earnings projected to outpace the market consistently over the long term.

**High-Tech Stock.** Securities of firms in high-technology industries, such as biotechnology, computers, electronics, lasers, medical devices, and robotics.

**Hybrid Security.** A security that possesses the characteristics of both stock and bonds, such as a convertible bond.

**Indenture.** The legal contract spelling out the terms and conditions between the issuer and bondholders.

**Index.** Compilation of performance for specific groupings of stocks or mutual funds, such as the Dow Jones Industrial Average, Standard & Poor's 500, etc.

**Insider.** Anyone having access to material corporate information. Most frequently used to refer to company officers, directors, and top management.

**Institutional Investor.** Investor organizations, such as pension funds and money managers, who trade large volumes of securities.

**Intrinsic Value.** The difference between the current market price of the underlying security and the striking price of a related option.

**IPO (Initial Public Offering).** The first public offering of a company's stock.

**Junk Bonds.** Bonds with ratings below investment grade.

**Leading Indicator.** An economic measurement that tends to accurately predict the future direction of the economy or stock market.

**Leverage.** The use of debt to finance a company's operations. Also, the use of debt by investors to increase the return on investment from securities transactions.

**Liquidity.** The degree of ease in which assets can be turned into readily available cash.

**Listed.** Investment securities that have met the listing requirements of a particular exchange.

**Maintenance Margin.** The minimum equity value that must be maintained in a margin account. Initial margin requirements include a minimum deposit of $2,000 before any credit can be extended. Current Regulation T rules require that a maintenance margin equal at least 50 percent of the market value of the margined positions.

**Margin.** The capital (in cash or securities) that an investor deposits with a broker to borrow additional funds to purchase securities.

**Margin Call.** A demand from a broker for additional cash or securities as collateral to bring the margin account back within maintenance limits.

**Mutual Fund.** An investment company that sells shares in itself to the investing public and uses the proceeds to purchase individual securities.

**NASDAQ.** National Association of Securities Dealers Automated Quotation System, which provides computerized quotes of market makers for stocks traded over the counter.

**Net Asset Value.** The quoted market value of a mutual fund share. Determined by dividing the closing market value of all securities owned by the mutual fund plus all other assets and liabilities by the total number of shares outstanding.

**Odd-Ball Theories.** Esoteric investment theories not readily explained by rational investment behavior or analysis. Examples include the Super Bowl, New York Mets, and Lunar investment theories.

**Option.** A security that gives the holder the right to purchase or sell a particular investment at a fixed price for a specified period of time.

**Out of the Money.** An option whose striking price is higher than the underlying security's current market price for a call option or whose striking price is lower than the current market price for a put option.

**Payout Ratio.** The percentage of a company's profit paid out in cash dividends.

**Portfolio.** The investment holdings of an individual or institutional investor, including stocks, bonds, options, money market accounts, etc.

**Price/Earnings Ratio.** Determined by dividing the stock's market price by its earnings per common share. Used as an indicator of company performance and in comparison with other stock investments and the overall market.

**Put Option.** A contract giving the holder the right to sell the underlying security at a specific price over a specified time frame.

**Quick Ratio.** The quick ratio is used to measure corporate liquidity. It is regarded as an improvement over the current ratio, which includes the usually not very liquid inventory. The quick ratio formula is computed as current assets less inventory divided by current liabilities.

**Range.** The high and low prices over which the security trades during a specific time frame: day, month, 52 weeks, etc.

**Relative Strength.** A comparison of a security's earnings or stock price strength in relation to other investments or indices.

**Risk.** The financial uncertainty that the actual return will vary from the expected return. Risk factors include inflation, deflation, interest rate risk, market risk, liquidity, default, etc.

**Secondary Market.** A market where previously issued securities trade, such as the New York Stock Exchange.

**Short Sale.** The sale of a security not yet owned in order to capitalize on an anticipated market price drop.

**Short Squeeze.** A rapid price rise forcing investors to cover their short positions. This drives the security price up even higher, often squeezing even more short investors.

**Special Situation.** An undervalued security with special circumstances, such as management change, new product, technological breakthrough, etc., favoring its return to better operating performance and higher prices.

**Spin-Off.** Shedding of a corporate subsidiary, division, or other operation via the issuance of shares in the new corporate entity.

**Split.** A change in the number of outstanding shares through the board of directors' action. The shareholder's equity remains the same; each shareholder receives the new stock in proportion to their holdings on the date of record. Dividends and earnings per share are adjusted to reflect the stock split.

**Standard & Poor's 500 (S&P 500).** Broad-based stock index composed of 400 industrial, 40 financial, 40 utility, and 20 transportation stocks.

**Striking Price.** The price at which an option or future contract can be executed according to the terms of the contract. Also called exercise price.

**10K, 10Q.** Annual and quarterly reports required by the Securities and Exchange Commission. They contain more in-depth financial and operating information then the annual and quarterly stockholder's reports.

**Technical Analysis.** Investment strategy that focuses on market and stock price patterns.

**Top-Down Investing.** Investment strategy starting with the overall economic scenario and then moving downward to consider industry and individual company investments.

**Total Return.** The return achieved by combining both the dividend/interest and capital appreciation earned on an investment.

**Trading Range.** The spread between the high and low prices for a given period.

**Turnaround.** A positive change in the fortunes of a company or industry. Turnarounds occur for a variety of reasons, such as economic upturn, new management, new product lines, strategic acquisition, etc.

**Underlying Security.** The security which may be bought or sold under the terms of an option agreement, warrant, etc.

**Undervalued Situation.** A security with a market value that does not fully value its potential or the true value of the company.

**Uptrend.** Upward movement in the market price of a stock.

**Volume.** The number of units of a security traded during a given time frame.

**Warrant.** An option to purchase a stated number of shares at a specified price within a specific time frame. Warrants are typically offered as sweeteners to enhance the marketability of stock or debt issues.

**Working Capital.** The difference between current assets and current liabilities.

**Yield.** An investor's return on investment from its interest- or dividend-paying capability.

# Index

# TWO GREAT
# INVESTMENT OFFERS!!!

**1.** *Gaming & Investments Quarterly* covering the explosive gambling, hotel and entertainment industries with in-depth analysis of unique common stock investment opportunities.

Regularly $75.00 annual subscription.
*Specially priced at $25.00 annual subscription.*

**2.** *Utility & Energy Portfolio.* Each issue packed with attractive common stock investment opportunities, discussions of where to find higher yields and safety plus coverage of major industry trends and key players.

Regularly $95.00 annual subscription includes annual investment roundup of every major U.S. utility.
*Specially priced at $35.00 annual subsciption.*

**BONUS** . . . Either subscription entitles you to a free copy of *Wall Street Words: The Basics and Beyond* by Richard J. Maturi, a $14.95 value.

- - - - - - - - - - - - - - - - - - - - - - - - - - - - - - -

Please send check or money order to:     OR use your Discover® Card:

**R. Maturi, Incorporated**         **Account No.:** _____
**1320 Curt Gowdy Drive**
**Cheyenne, WY  82009**          **Expiration Date:** _____

                    **Signature:** _____

_____ *Gaming and Investments Quarterly* @ **$25.00.  SAVE $50.00!**

_____ *Utility and Energy Portfolio* @ **$35.00.    SAVE $60.00!**

Name _____

Street _____

City _____ State _____ Zip _____

Phone (    ) _____

# About the Publisher

PROBUS PUBLISHING COMPANY

Probus Publishing Company fills the informational needs of today's business professional by publishing authoritative, quality books on timely and relevant topics, including:

- Investing
- Futures/Options Trading
- Banking
- Finance
- Marketing and Sales
- Manufacturing and Project Management
- Personal Finance, Real Estate, Insurance and Estate Planning
- Entrepreneurship
- Management

Probus books are available at quantity discounts when purchased for business, educational or sales promotional use. For more information, please call the Director, Corporate/Institutional Sales at 1-800-998-4644, or write:

Director, Corporate/Institutional Sales
Probus Publishing Company
1925 N. Clybourn Avenue
Chicago, Illinois 60614
FAX (312) 868-6250